Resources for Teaching Creative Writing

Resources available for download

Worksheets from this book are available online at
www.continuumbooks.com/resources/9780826443540.

Please visit the link and register with us to receive your password and
access to these downloadable resources.

If you experience any problems accessing the resources, please contact
Continuum at info@continuumbooks.com

Also available from Continuum

Teaching Creative Writing – Graeme Harper
100 Ideas for Teaching Drama – Johnnie Young
100+ Ideas for Managing Behaviour – Johnnie Young
Resources for Teaching French – Gill James

Resources for Teaching Creative Writing

Johnnie Young

continuum

Continuum International Publishing Group

The Tower Building   80 Maiden Lane, Suite 704

11 York Road   New York NY 10038

London SE1 7NX

www.continuumbooks.com

British Library Cataloguing-in-Publication Data
A catalogue record for this book is available from the British Library.

ISBN: 978-0-8264-0992-8 (paperback)

Library of Congress Cataloging-in-Publication Data
Young, Johnnie.
 Resources for teaching creative writing / Johnnie Young.
    p. cm.
 ISBN 978-0-8264-4354-0 (pbk. : alk. paper)
 1. Creative writing (Secondary education) I. Title.

 LB1631.Y68 2009
 808'.0420712--dc22

 2009009348

Designed and typeset by Kenneth Burnley, Wirral, Cheshire
Printed and bound in Great Britain by

This book is dedicated to my wife Sylvie

and my children Edward, Julie and William.

It is also dedicated to the memory of my mother and father.

Contents

Introduction

The key ideas behind this book are based on my attempts during 17 years of teaching to encourage students to write imaginatively and creatively. I have found that most students may find themselves unsure and lacking in confidence in the early stages of the process. To be given a writing task such as: 'Write about a day in the life of a golf ball' may fire up the creative juices of the teacher, but English teachers have had a lot of experience in firing up their own creative juices. What I have found that most students need is an example of a finished product so that they can set their 'mental co-ordinates': a set of suggestions to prompt them into action and in some cases a step by step approach with teacher guidance and encouragement. The crucial thing is the actual examples they are shown. If the example is too sophisticated (for example, a description of a character from a Dickens novel) this creates a distancing between what they see before them and what they feel they are capable of writing. Examples are therefore required which bridge this gap. Many teachers rewrite examples themselves, from literature, to fulfil this need to bridge the gap. But this takes an awful lot of time.

This book provides 60 ready-to-use examples. The examples are not taken from well-known works of literature. I have, in fact, written all the examples myself, based on my own experiences in the classroom and seeing what engages the students' attention, holds their interest and allows them to think with a 'I can do that' attitude. Once their interest is engaged with the example of a 'finished product' the suggestion lists give the students choice for the next step, and then trigger their own creative processes. I have found that this unlocks amazing things. Students want to write creatively. They love it when it goes well. They just need the right tools with which to do it.

The book is organized into ten thematic sections. Within the thematic sections is a wide range of writing types and skills ranging from dramatic monologues to poetry. The book balances the requirement to teach creative writing to specifically help with the KS4 and KS5 syllabuses and the desire to 'open out' the field of creative writing to explore its many aspects for the students' pure pleasure and joy of writing creatively.

The book will be appropriate to any secondary school teacher who wants to teach creative writing to an age range of 14 to 18 years old.

The general layout is to show the Teacher Notes on the left-hand side and an accompanying photocopiable resource Student Worksheet on the right.

The Teacher Notes include all the information needed to provide a well-balanced and challenging lesson. Each idea begins with a summary of key skills so that the teacher can quickly place the activity to a particular area of the National Curriculum. There is then a starter, a chunked main phase and a plenary. For each one there is an idea for homework and suggestions to develop the work, if desired, by the teacher. A particular feature is to include, for each idea, a special focus and development exercise for the KS4 and KS5 syllabus.

I do hope that this book helps you to deliver some great lessons. There is nothing better than hearing a student read his or her own creative writing with a sense of pleasure and pride. Sometimes, as busy teachers, we don't realize just how deep that pleasure goes. I've been teaching long enough now to have the privilege of meeting students in the street who refer to stories they enjoyed writing decades ago. Isn't that great! They may not have become famous authors but they produced something which they were proud of. What a job this is where a bit of creative writing done in your classroom will be so memorable for them in years to come. I really wish you the best in delivering lessons that can make such an impression on your students' lives.

Acknowledgements

I would like to thank my editor Christina Garbutt whose tireless help, patience and expertise are greatly appreciated.

Section A: Realize a Dream

Key skills

1. Writing travel diary notes.

Starter

Ask students to write down seven reasons why someone would write a diary. Then ask the students to write a list of the places in the world they would like to visit. Ask them to explain why.

Main phase

Part 1
Read through with students the adventure travel diary in the worksheet.

Part 2
Read through and discuss with the students the important features of a diary entry, in Part 2 of the worksheet.

Part 3
Ask students to write their own imaginative travel diary using as many features as they can and basing the style on the example. They may wish to choose a scenario from the list, in Part 3 of the worksheet.

Plenary

Do a question-and-answer session around the class to recap on diary features.

Suggestions for homework

Ask students to research and find an example of a travel diary. Ask them to bring it in and read an extract to the class. It would be good to hear a range and variety of entries.

Suggestions for development of this work

Ask students to research and find an example of a diary entry from a travel diary. Students to then copy it out and annotate with a different colour the identified diary features.

Extended exercise to develop a KS4 focus based on this work

Students to produce a storyboard of a journey with extracts written under each picture in diary entry style. For example: the first picture may show a boat setting sail. The diary 'caption' might read: 'We set off at 10.30 am on 9 August. Weather ideal with a strong south-westerly wind.' The second picture may show a close-up of the cooking equipment in the galley. The caption may read: 'Although small, the galley's cooker was excellent for most requirements. Our first break was two hours into the journey when we had soup and rolls.' And so on. The entries can then be checked back to the diary entry features list in worksheet Part 3, and adjusted if necessary.

Extended exercise to develop a KS5 focus based on this work

Ask students to research and find an example of a travel diary. Ask them to bring it in and read an extract to the class. They then recast the writing into a letter to a friend. A commentary is then written to compare the two styles of writing. So each student will find their own travel diary example, recast the writing into letter form and then write their own individual commentary to show the comparison of the two writing styles. It would be a good idea to then discuss the outcomes with each other.

Part 1

An example of a diary entry

Background

I had always wanted to sail in an old traditional ketch type sailing ship around Cape Horn. After months of planning, my journey began. The highlight of the adventure was the rounding of the Cape. Here is an extract from my diaries:

Day 20. 11.30 am   Cape Horn

It is 11.30 in the morning and we have finally arrived at Cape Horn. This is the stretch of sea which joins the Atlantic to the Pacific Ocean. The waves are at one moment towering above me and then the next we're flung high up with a smooth powerful energy onto the crest, at that very moment I caught a glimpse of the Cape itself. A huge grey mass of unforgiving stone, appearing like a dark shrouded demon through the rain and the spray. My friend and crew member Paul is suffering terribly with his stomach. I tried to direct his attention to the Cape but he is being violently sick over the side. I've never felt so scared in my life as I cling to my harness and brace the buffeting in every direction, drenched by wave after wave and drinking in nothing but salt. I feel like an unwelcome guest in a strange world, not helped by me trying to take a picture just now and having my camera snatched from my hand and flung over the side by fearsome watery fingers! And yet, although I'd been told again and again that this is the most dangerous stretch of waters in the world, I feel an odd sensation of calm power deep inside. Despite everything, I've overcome my fear and I've actually done it. From the days when I first looked at maps at school I had wanted this adventure. Now I am here I feel proud of my own courage. There may not be a photo to show when I get home, but the image of all this will be scarred into my mind for ever.

Part 2

Here are some important features of a diary entry:

1. It starts with a date and perhaps a place.
2. It is written in the first person as in 'I' or 'We'.
3. It recounts events in a logical order.
4. It will include, at times, how the writer feels.
5. It may include some descriptions of what is seen or experienced.
6. The tense of the writing is very often in the present.

Part 3

Have a go at writing your own travel diary entry. It may include excitement and adventure or it may include a straightforward description of a visit somewhere. If you want help starting, use the ideas below which you may then continue with. Try to include some of the features from the list.

Possible scenarios:

1. Antarctica

Day 20. 9 am. I emerge from my warm cabin into the frozen crisp air and see a sight which leaves me stunned . . . Hundreds of penguins, looking like men in evening suits slowly waddle towards the icy cold ocean . . . CONTINUE.

2. Deep sea trawler fishing

Day 2. Midnight. Why did I agree to go on this crazy 'adventure holiday'? I love fishing but this is ridiculous! We're hauling in a massive catch and the fish are squirming about all over the place. I've never seen so many fish. The captain has told me to keep clear of the chains. The storm is so fierce that sometimes you feel like you're in a lift as you're pushed suddenly up and then dropped down.

3. Paris

Perhaps visiting with friends and having a good time seeing the sights.

4. Egypt

A trip down the Nile and a visit to the Pyramids.

5. Australia

A journey through the 'outback'.

Adventure Travel Diary, Cape Horn   **WORKSHEET**

Key skills

1. Writing a radio interview transcript.
2. Role play.

Starter

Ask students to write out their ambitions.

Main phase

Part 1

Read through the example radio interview called 'How I achieved my dream', found in Part 1 of the worksheet.

Part 2

Ask students to write out a transcript of questions and answers with members of the public phoning in with questions.

Part 3

Ask students to work out a situation where they achieve their dream ambition. It could be large or small scale. The important thing is that it is a dream to them. Remind them to imagine it in great detail. Then ask them to write out a radio interview transcript in the style of the example, in Part 1 of the worksheet.

Plenary

Arrange for students to read out their interviews in a role-play style, working in pairs, and reading to the rest of the group.

Suggestions for homework

Ask students to research a person who they admire who has achieved a great deal. Ask them to then write out an imaginary interview with that person. A list of people who have achieved a great deal is in Part 2 of the worksheet. The person may still be alive or may be from history. The interview will be the same. The students, working in pairs, could then present their interviews to the class and then, perhaps, take part in a question-and-answer session to show their knowledge of the person being interviewed.

Suggestions for development of this work

Arrange for students to carry out their own research about a famous or influential figure in history and write out their findings, in their own words, to be presented in a booklet. The information should then conclude with a summary of key points about how that person achieved his or her dream ambition.

Extended exercise to develop a KS4 focus based on this work

Ask students to write an article called 'Achieve your Dream' for a teenage magazine to include examples and advice from successful people. Part 2 of the students' worksheet includes a list of successful people. Write in the style of a teenage magazine article.

Extended exercise to develop a KS5 focus based on this work

Ask students to write a commentary on their own work for a radio interview transcript.

Include:

1. How you found out about what to say.
2. What you imagined the audience for this interview to be.
3. How you rewrote the interview to get it just right for the audience you had in mind.
4. What you have learned by listening to radio interviews of this type.

Part 1
How I achieved my dream

Example radio interview transcript. The interviewer is Sue.

Sue: We are delighted to have with us today Mike Kennedy who's kindly agreed to tell us about his life. Welcome Mike to Radio Dreamer. We're delighted to have you with us.

Mike: Hello. I must say it's great to be here. Thanks for inviting me.

Sue: For those of our listeners who have not heard about you, could I just summarize what you have achieved. You founded a worldwide network of special youth centres which are all part of the Michael Kennedy International Youth Centre Movement. First, can we go back to your beginnings. Tell us about your early life. You were born into poverty, weren't you?

Mike: Yes, that's right. The area where I grew up was one of the most deprived areas in the UK. I had to borrow an outside tin bath from the neighbours, to wash in. The water was available from a tap down the lane. The homes were constructed a little like sheds. All my clothes were hand-me-downs. That sort of thing.

Sue: Tell us about your school days.

Mike: Terrible. I was forced to eat cold, lumpy mashed potatoes. The teachers hit us frequently to get us to work. I found it very hard to learn to read and write because I remember a large lady standing over me, menacingly, as I tried to match a picture card to a word, and my hands started to shake with fear. 'You're thick if you can't match that simple picture!' she yelled. Of course my confidence collapsed and I was put in special classes.

Sue: But you caught up, didn't you?

Mike: Yes. I realized that if I worked twice as hard as everybody else I might catch up. In fact I not only caught up but I overtook them.

Sue: You now hold an Honours degree don't you?

Mike: Yes, that's right. I'm very proud of that.

Sue: How did the foundation start?

Mike: I realized that a lot of crime and trouble with young people was due to a lack of things to get meaningfully involved in. For a lot of young people, standing on street corners was their evening's activity. I started asking teenagers what it was they really wanted. After a year I came up with a blueprint for a youth centre that would cater for the majority of the needs of the teenagers and keep them occupied and entertained.

Sue: The main hurdle must have been the financing?

Mike: Yes. I lay in bed at night wondering about that for a long time. Then one day I was out walking and an idea hit me. Supposing I could sell the benefits of such a youth centre to a whole community and prove that it was good news for everyone, wouldn't they be prepared to support it by sharing the cost? I figured that as a resident myself I would be happy to give a few pounds to help set this up.

Sue: And it worked out.

Mike: But, it's one thing to have an idea. It's quite another to get people to part with their money. Anyway, after years of knocking on doors, talking to local people and getting the idea well known in the area, I eventually got the funding to design and build a youth centre which the teenagers think is brilliant. Once it was set up and running, everyone benefited.

Sue: But building one youth centre is one thing, how did you go from that to a world wide network of over 5,000 youth centres?

Mike: I was sitting in a fast-food outlet one day thinking about how you could go anywhere in the world and get the exact service from this chain of outlets. I did a lot of research and learned about a thing called a 'franchise'. Basically you design a business model which works perfectly and you replicate it. I managed to write out the details of a perfect working model for a youth centre and with help from some business sponsors managed to get a lot of different towns interested. Once it was set up and running in this country the next step was to go international. There is scope for adaptations and refinements to be made but the basic model remains the same.

Sue: There are now over five million teenagers around the world who benefit from your youth centres, aren't there?

Mike: Yes, that's right. I'm pleased to say that many millions more benefit in the communities they serve.

Sue: To sum up then Mike, if you had to give the key secrets of how you lifted yourself from a situation of poverty to a position of worldwide acclaim, what would they be?

Mike: Hard work, persistence, careful preparation and the ability to convince people about your ideas. Also, expect obstacles in life. Nothing ever worth doing is easy.

Sue: Well, thank you Mike from the Michael Kennedy International Youth Centre Movement. Mike has agreed to answer phone-ins with your questions, and the lines are now open.

Part 2

A list of people who have achieved a great deal.

1. Richard Branson, who from scratch set up and developed a huge business empire.
2. Paul McCartney, who was a founder member of The Beatles, one of the world's most influential pop groups.
3. Neil Armstrong, the first person to walk on the moon.
4. Jim Carrey, a star of many popular comedy films.

Radio Interview – Realize a Dream Ambition **WORKSHEET**

Key skills

1. Writing in a 'flow of consciousness' style.

Starter

Ask students to think of a dream they've had and write out an account of it.

Discuss with them this question: 'What are the difficulties of writing about a dream?'

Main phase

Part 1

Read through, with the students, the example of a written account of a dream.

Draw attention to the following features:

1. Sentences run on in a flow of consciousness style.
2. Images which seem familiar change into other things.
3. Time and space become distorted.
4. Things change colour and size.
5. Inanimate objects can become alive.
6. Look out for useful connecting phrases like 'I found myself'.
7. Things don't have to make sense as far as content goes, but the language itself must be logical and interesting, making use of poetic qualities where possible.
8. Focus, at times, on tiny details and bring them alive.
9. Give the writing a structure using paragraphs and link one little episode to another to provide a flow of action.

Part 2

Discuss the chart of prompt ideas and encourage the students to have a go at writing their own dreams based on the style of the example given.

Plenary

Ask students to list three things which make a piece of writing about a dream interesting to listen to.

Suggestions for homework

Ask students to research and find a painting by a Surrealist painter like Salvador Dali or Rene Magritte. Remind them to look for one which has a dreamlike quality. Set them the task of describing the picture in detail and bringing in the description with a copy of the painting.

Suggestions for development of this work

Provide a set of copies of Surrealist paintings which contain dreamlike qualities. Ask students to write out a dream based on the painting.

Ask students to produce illustrations based on their own writings about dreams.

Extended exercise to develop a KS4 focus based on this work

Ask students to research symbols in dreams and select five. If they type out 'dream symbols' on an internet search engine they will find a wealth of ideas to choose from. Write an explanation of what the symbols may signify and then write out a dream using the symbols as images in the writing.

Extended exercise to develop a KS5 focus based on this work

Ask students to write out a description of a dream in the form of a dramatic monologue. They can then think about a performance of the monologue, and consideration can be given to how the audience will experience the performance. Then arrange for them to give a performance to the class. After the performance, members of the class (the audience) can write a response to how they experienced the performance.

Part 1
Example of a dream

As the pink mist cleared, I saw my brown cuddly teddy bear, sitting on the end of my bed. I went to pick it up and heard a strange slushing sound accompanied a dizzy spinning whirl of lights and colours and then I found myself sitting in the arms of a huge real alive bear and we were perched at the top of the Golden Gate Bridge, swaying in the wind. I felt that all-embracing feeling you get when you're about to fall; and I did fall! I felt a terrifying rush of air. I clenched my muscles and waited for the impact.

But no crash came. Instead I was lying on a cold stone floor looking up at an arched window. Birds were singing outside and I tried to lift my head but couldn't. I felt my hand slowly rising and falling to a gentle rhythm by my side. I looked. My hand was on the belly of a fully grown leopard. He was sleeping soundly. I closed my eyes and drew my hand away, carefully, slowly. I opened my eyes.

I had been whisked away and was now on a wide white sandy beach. On the beach was a full-size mirror. I looked into the mirror. My face looked fine but behind, reflected in the mirror, was a shape looming towards me. I swung round and a smiling fisherman with a huge beard put out his hand to shake mine. I felt a huge rush of energy at this point and ran off with all the speed I could manage. As I glanced behind I clearly saw that the fisherman was driving his tractor along the sands towards me. His face had changed to anger. His beard had become pink candyfloss. The tractor was made of pure gold and the headlamps were massive diamonds. Behind him, attached to a fishing line was a fish which grew bigger and bigger and pulled the tractor down into the sand. I kept running but when I glanced back for the last time I saw golden bubbles of sand engulfing the tractor. I ran and ran. I stopped in my tracks. There in front of me was a pair of pink ballerina's shoes, but stuffed into them were big red blistered feet. I looked up and there was the fisherman. His head had changed to a gold sculpture and the expression was a frozen enigmatic smile.

Part 2

Write your own dream. Use ideas from the prompt below to get you started, if you need a prompt. Introduce as many of your own ideas as you can. Change and adapt them to create interesting effects.

Images, objects, people and things	What they might do	Setting	What you do and what this links onto
Shampoo in a bath bubbles up the water to a green colour and the bubbles spread all over the bath and out into the garden.	The bubbles make the plants in the garden sway and dance.	The garden could be bathed in bright sunshine but as the plants start to dance a snow blizzard strikes up. The sound of a distant drum is heard.	You might frantically try to stop the bath water by turning off the taps. You then become sucked into the plug hole and experience an adventure as you enter into the centre of the earth.

Writing about a Dream   **WORKSHEET**

Key skills

1. Letter-writing technique.
2. Persuasive writing.
3. Writing to explain and describe.

Starter

Ask students to describe, in writing, and with a time limit of ten minutes, their ambitions and dreams.

Main phase

Part 1

Read through with the students the advertisement on the worksheet for a competition which appeared in a magazine. Discuss.

Part 2

Read through with the students the example of a letter for entry into the competition. Discuss key features.

Part 3

Go through the features of the letter and ask students to write their own letters to the editor about their own dreams.

Plenary

Ask students to read their letters to their partners and vice versa. Partners to make constructive comments to help each other improve.

Suggestions for homework

Research the autobiography (or biography) of an admired person and trace how they developed from where they were to where they got to. Write out the journey in a series of bullet points which show the stages of the progression.

Suggestions for development of this work

Arrange for the class to work as a group and create a display which includes the examples and a variety of 'dreams and ambitions' from the group. Include in the display key words and symbols and illustrations. The overall impression will be an exciting shared vision of the future. It could have a bold title such as: 'Class dreams for the future'.

Extended exercise to develop a KS4 focus based on this work

Ask students to carry out some research (allow perhaps a week) to find out what type of career they would love to have. Encourage them to find the information from a variety of sources and collect it together in note form. Then the student is to write out, in diagram form, using symbols, key words and illustrations and small extracts of writing, how someone may achieve that particular dream. So, for example: 'How to achieve the dream of being a fighter pilot'.

They then imagine that they have achieved that particular dream and they write a comment, as if they were experiencing it, to finish off the article. This last section might have the sub-heading of: 'Let's hear a few words from John who is himself a fighter pilot . . .' Once the whole class have done this, their work may be compiled and bound together in one book entitled: *How to Achieve your Dreams*.

Extended exercise to develop a KS5 focus based on this work

Carry out the exercise in KS4 Focus above. In addition, have students choose one of the dreams and write a script for a short radio play which shows the successful progression of a student from school to achievement of a dream. The radio play is then 'performed' to the class. The students then write an essay to answer this question: 'Compare how the audience's visualization of a future dream differs between their reading descriptions of it and hearing a dramatized version of it'

Part 1

Dream competition

The editor invites you, the reader, to write about your dream and ambitions. The writing must explain and describe in detail what your ambition is. The clearer the judges can picture it in their imaginations, the more chance you have of winning! The writing must be set out in the form of a letter to the editor at the address shown below. The closing date for entries is the 1st of next month. The letters will be judged by a panel of judges and winners will be notified within two months of the closing date.

A stamped addressed envelope must be enclosed if you would like your entry returned.

The prizes are:

- *First Prize:* An adventure holiday to Africa for two weeks with all expenses paid. Up to a maximum of four people will be paid for.
- *Second Prize:* £500 in cash.
- *Third Prize:* £100 in cash.

The rules are provided inside the back page of this magazine. So what are you waiting for? Get writing . . .

The address to write to is:

The Editor, Dreamy Dreams Magazine, The Dream Competition, Gunfloat House, High Street, Cranford CR4 3LD.

Part 2

Dear Editor,

My ambition is to own my own Alpine mountain chalet. I would like to be able to run it like a hotel during the holiday season. To be able to do this, and to offer a great holiday package, I would also love to become a ski instructor.

When, several years ago, I went on a skiing holiday organised by my school, I caught the skiing 'bug'. Since then I have often thought about the place. It has now firmly become my ambition and dream, to involve myself in the ski scene.

I can visualize my life a few years on from now. I know this will sound as if I'm wearing a pair of rosy coloured spectacles, but here it is. The alarm clock will sound (an Alpine cuckoo clock of course). I will leap out of bed and into the luxury shower. My partner will help me make breakfast for ten hungry, appreciative guests. Can you imagine them seated around a huge pine table, chatting about their plans to ski for the day, laughing as they remember the fun they had yesterday. They will be enjoying home-baked bread made by me; they will be sipping hot coffee. Once all the breakfast is sorted I shall escort them to one of the ski sites (nearby) and teach them how to ski.

Can you imagine the sight of the mountains? The invigorating feel of the place? The fir trees; the distance peaks picking up the sunshine; the air clean and sweet?

After a day's skiing we will return to the chalet and sit round a roaring fire eating magnificient food. I will feel the warmth of appreciation from my guests. They will enjoy their holiday with us so much that they will be returning year after year.

Is this just a dream hanging in the air? Not at all! I have already begun the process which will take me to those Italian Alps. I have enrolled at a local indoor ski slope club and I am learning as much as I can about the art and craft of skiing. I am studying case histories of people who have actually done this for real. I'm even learning to speak Italian. I know it will take a long time for it to happen, but I am not for the quick fix. I believe that you must work hard for anything worth having.

I believe that a dream can and will come true if certain conditions are met. First of all, you must have a burning passion and desire. My friends think I'm mad. All I do is talk about skiing. Second, you must have a plan which will take you where you want to go. Inch by Inch. Step by step. All the things I'm learning now will help me later. Knowledge is power. Then, third, is the tricky little matter of money. Well, I've solved that one too! I've got myself a part-time Saturday job and most of the money is being paid into a bank account which I have opened. I know it might take a long time, but seriously, don't you think my dream is unstoppable?

On my bedroom wall is a chart and each time I do something towards my dream, I write it down on the chart. I've stuck some lovely pictures of Alpine scenes there. Whenever I feel a little downhearted I glance at my chart.

Maybe I'll never achieve absolutely everything I want. After all, the Alpine mountains reach right up to the sky. But if you ever did see my chart on the wall, you'll see a quotation I've copied from an old poet: 'A man's dream must always be beyond his reach, or what's a heaven for?'

Yours sincerely

Philip Luckin

Key skills

1. Writing poetry.
2. Exploring forms of poetry.
3. Exploring the language of poetry.
4. Using a method to write a poem.

Starter

Ask students to discuss with a partner a dream place of excitement and wonder which they would like to journey into and explore.

Main phase

Part 1

Read through the poem with the students.

Discuss the following points:

1. The poem rhymes in couplets. The effect of this is to move the pace on briskly. This sort of form is suitable when a journey is being described and you want to give the reader a sense of movement from one place to another.
2. The rhyming couplets help create a regular, fast-paced rhythm.
3. The descriptions of things on the journey are impressions only. They are like visual glimpses which allow the imagination of the audience to do the rest. For example: 'red guitar' allows a very detailed and rich image to appear in the imagination.
4. One image quickly follows another and the reader gets the impression of being bombarded with fleeting images, just as you would on a journey of discovery.
5. The land has certain mysterious and dreamlike qualities. Some descriptions are deliberately left vague, for example: 'wonderous things'.
6. There is a variety of sights and experiences which include landscape, buildings, plants, animals and people.
7. There is movement and action, for example: 'dancing, singing, shouting'.
8. Most of the rhyming couplets contain a balance: for example:

   Plants with massive purple flowers,
   I could have smelt their perfume for hours.

9. Structure of poem: the narrator sets out a clear intention at the start, describes the journey in the bulk of the poem and then makes a general summing-up comment at the end.

Part 2

Ask students to have a try at writing a poem in rhyming couplets which describes impressions of a journey in the style of the example given.

They may wish to use the suggestions and method as set out in Part 2 of the worksheet.

Plenary

Students to read out a few of the poems to the class.

Suggestions for homework

Take home the poem begun in the class and edit and rewrite it to enhance it.

Suggestions for development of this work

Students to research and find pictures of fascinating places and a poem to be written about it using the method set out in Part 2.

Extended exercise to develop a KS4 focus based on this work

Students to find a variety of poems with different rhythm and rhyme schemes. Students to find out the technical names for different forms of poems and report back to the class.

Extended exercise to develop a KS5 focus based on this work

Students to discuss, imagine and make notes on a fantasy land full of excitement and wonder. They then write a detailed prose description and then a poem composed of rhyming couplets. The two are then compared and a report written to answer this question: 'What are the different experiences felt by the reader when reading prose compared to poetry?'

Part 1

My Adventure Dream

In the morning I was gripped with a thought
And by lunch time I had bought
All the things within my grasp
And packed my food and my new flask.
Mid afternoon saw me venture out,
And happy with my new boots I had no doubt,
That I would keep exploring right on through,
The evening and the night time too.
Although my rucksack felt heavier by the mile
I had on my face an adventurer's smile.
When the time came to put up my tent
I realized that I had spent
Countless hours exploring alone
And not once had I a desire to moan.
Once a bright lake, with pleasure I had passed,
Once, to get away from a snake, I ran fast.
Deep caverns I'd explored with feelings of fear
With a sense of excitement suddenly near.
The fantasy world I'd entered into
Was full of wonder, and scary things too!

I saw flying fish with silvery wings
And rugged coastlines with wondrous things.
Plants with massive purple flowers
I could have smelt their perfume for hours!
Crumbling towers from ancient time
Inscriptions on walls which seemed to rhyme.
Landscapes sweeping to oceans blue,
Undergrowth so thick you couldn't get through.
Ornate palaces adorned with splendour,
Roaming beasts, some fierce, some tender.
Strange men in alleys playing board games
Children singing and calling out names.
A bright red guitar played fast and loud
A swaying happy singing crowd.
Women, clothes flowing, performing a dance,
Sculptures fixed in a strange silent trance.
My list of impressions is precious to me
And lives in my memory, I hope you can see
Some of the magic you get when you strive
To keep the adventurous spirit alive!

Part 2

Suggestions for a process for writing a poem

Step 1

Write out a 'map' in rough outline of places you would like to visit and things and experiences you would encounter on the way.

Step 2

For each important place along the way write a rhyming couplet.

Imagine, for example, that in your poem you wish to cross a river. First of all write down a set of questions so that you can imaginatively explore in detail the situation. For example:

a) How deep is the river?
b) What colour is the water?
c) What is on either side of the river?
d) What temperature is the water?
e) Is it fast flowing or still?
f) Is there a smell? How strong?
g) Who are you with? Alone or a crowd?
h) Do you want to get across the river easily or with great difficulty?
i) Are you carrying anything?
j) What time of day is it?
k) What is the weather like?
l) Does any creature lurk in the water?

Step 3

The next step is to answer these questions in ordinary prose writing. For example:

The river is very deep, murky green in colour and there are trees on either bank. The water is warm and flows with furious energy. There is a strong smell of rotting flesh. I am on my own, having great difficulty crossing carrying a heavy load. It has become dusk and a storm is brewing. Against my leg I feel a large soft creature move slowly.

Step 4

Experiment with writing a rhyming couplet using that information. Importantly, you don't have to use all the information but you have got enough 'raw material' to provide choices to work with.

Example:

The river is dark, murky and green and its power is grasping at me,

I flounder and gasp with my heavy load and fear what I cannot see.

Step 5

Experiment with reading the lines out loud and edit until the rhythm flows smoothly.

Key skills

1. Writing imaginatively.

Starter

Ask students to think of a science fiction book or film they have seen. They are to spend ten minutes writing an explanation of what happens in it.

Main phase

Part 1

Read through with the students the example of the Science Fiction Writing in Part 1 of the worksheet. Discuss. Ask students to identify any features they noticed of science fiction writing.

Part 2

Ask students to write their own science fiction short story using the style of the example and getting a suggested idea (if they need one) from the list in Part 2 of the worksheet.

Plenary

Students to read their science fiction accounts to each other in pairs.

Suggestions for homework

Students to take home their science fiction account and imagine it was to be made into a film. Ask them to produce a poster to advertise it.

Suggestions for development of this work

Arrange for the whole class to put together a collaborative science fiction story. It could be organized like this:

1. Five students to write five different science fiction settings which could be used in the story.
2. Five students to invent and describe five different science fiction characters to be used.
3. Five students to design and sketch five different modes of transport which could be used in the story.
4. Five students to imagine five different things which could happen in the story.
5. Five students to use all of the above to write the story, in five sections:
   a) Start.
   b) Development.
   c) Problem one explored and resolved.
   d) Problem two explored and resolved.
   e) Conclusion.
6. Five students to work as advisers and editors and put the finished story together.

Extended exercise to develop a KS4 focus based on this work

Carry out the exercise described in 'Suggestion for development of this work' above, but all the work to be done as an individual student, taking a couple of weeks to complete.

Extended exercise to develop a KS5 focus based on this work

Ask students to carry out the exercise in the KS4 Focus above and in addition write an essay to answer this question: 'Based on your own experience of putting together a science fiction story, what have you found to be the most important aspects of a science fiction story?'

Part 1

Out of time

I have been asked to write a report, to put on record the strange events of four years ago.

As a young student I took a particular interest in science. I managed to get into a university and took a degree and then specialized in a research degree on the subject of Metamurphchronoultrozonics. If that area of science is unfamiliar to you, do not worry, only two people really know about it, the professor who invented it and myself, who proved the truth of it. I will seek to make everything clear.

My professor was an absolutely fascinating man. His name was Professor Herbert Butler and his drive and determination fired my interest and imagination. To cut a very long story short, he believed that it was possible not only to travel through time but also 'out of time'. The work he began, I continued. My researches took me to far-flung places around the world and I consulted and studied thousands of ancient texts. At one point I was so involved with my studies that I worked 60 hours with hardly a break. Most days were 20-hour days. I did try to get help from various research academics, but apart from Professor Butler nobody would take my research seriously.

Five years ago tragedy struck. The professor was researching some ancient text in a Turkish library when a huge bookcase fell on him and he was crushed. I flew over and visited him in his hospital bed. He whispered a few words in my ear before he died: 'guss . . . set . . . hid . . . you . . . only.' I thought he was delirious. Obviously I was deeply upset but more determined than ever to continue his work.

The words he whispered to me remained a frustrating mystery for nearly a year until one day, when I was buying a new notebook, the girl behind the counter asked me if I wanted a notebook with a special section at the back to store loose papers known as a gusset. Then it hit me! Of course! The dying words the professor had said must have referred to a notebook he had. I was able to search his belongings (which his will had ordered to be kept in a bank vault) when I made a fascinating discovery.

There was a notebook with a special gusset and inside it were strange pieces of paper scrawled with all manner of drawings and calculations and what looked like maps. After several months of painstaking work, the information which the professor had left steered me onto a path of incredible discovery.

I won't go into too much detail but I was able to collect together various chemical compounds and other things and the time arrived for me to undertake an experiment. The procedure itself must remain a secret but I was able to enter 'out of time' for exactly one hour.

The place was the same but everything, except me, was frozen in time. I could walk out into the street and see everyone – cars, animals, everything – completely frozen still. I touched one man and he was warm and soft but at the same time absolutely like a statue. Apparently I had entered 'out of time'. After exactly one hour of normal time (my watch still worked) I returned to normal existence.

I told a few close friends about it but the reaction was always the same. They thought I had been working too hard and had hallucinated! I needed some sort of proof.

I tried out various combinations of the experiment when, four years ago, I entered into a frozen world of 'out of time' but 1,000 years into the future!

I am the only person on this planet who knows what the future will look like. I had exactly one hour to find out. First of all the sun in the sky looked exactly the same. The sky itself looked exactly the same. So what was different? Just about everything else. People had no hair on their heads and were mainly tall and thin. They all seemed to be of the same age (about 25 years old at a guess) and they all seemed to wear the same expression of happiness on their faces. They all wore the same clothes. These were silver and white apron-like things. The material was incredibly thin! On each wrist was a watch-like thing but on closer examination seemed to be connected through their skin to the bone!

There were no buildings at all and the ground was a silky, shiny thing. Goodness only knows where they lived! There are obviously thousands of other things to tell but I have confined myself to the most important.

I have discovered that my system will allow just one more 'out of time' journey. If I have any more I will be badly injured. I have decided to use my last 'out of time' experience to go back in time. I need some evidence that this thing actually is real to convince the world about what I've done.

Part 2

Suggestions for writing a science fiction account.

1. Describe and explain the experience of 'Out of time' which takes you back in time.
2. Describe a journey where you are made microscopically small.
3. Describe a journey where you visit another planet.
4. Describe an experience where you venture deep underground and discover a lost civilization.
5. Describe an experience where you visit the sea bed and find some unexpected creatures.
6. Describe the experience of being made into a giant as tall as the Eiffel Tower for just one hour.
7. Imagine you invented a machine that could duplicate people. Describe your adventures.
8. Imagine that you found a way to make fantastically nice food out of mud. Describe what happens.
9. You invent a way for anyone to buy a personal 'force field' which is invisible and protects you from anything. Describe your experiences with it.
10. You find a way to change someone's personality at the flick of a switch. Write about what might happen.

Science Fiction   **WORKSHEET**

Section B: Some Elements of Writing

Key skills

1. Short story writing using restricted minimal information.
2. Making creative connections.

Starter

Ask students to write down five examples of 'settings' for a story. Explain to the students that the 'setting' has two elements, the 'when' and the 'where'. For example, a cave, 1,000 years ago.

Main phase

1. Read through the example on the worksheet (Task 1) which introduces four elements of a story. Read through the story which is written from those four elements and discuss how they are used. Explain that by keeping things to just four elements it tightens the focus of the story.
2. Task 2. Ask students to read the examples of four elements and ask them to write a story using one of them.
3. Ask students to come up with their own four elements and then write a story using them.

Plenary

Students can read their stories to the class. Encourage a discussion about which parts of their stories work well and which parts could be developed and suggestions for how this might happen.

Suggestions for homework

Ask students to draw up four columns on a piece of A4 paper and write four headings:

1. Setting.
2. Main character.
3. Essence of story line.
4. Main object.

Then write three elements under each heading and finally 'pick and mix' an element from each heading and write a story keeping to those elements.

Suggestions for development of this work

Produce a set of colour-coded element cards, one colour for each of the four elements. Have a set of each and shuffle each set. Give each student a set of the range of four colours. They will be randomly shuffled but will have one of each colour to work with. Ask them to write a story based on their element cards. It fires creativity!

Examples which could be used:

1. Red setting cards:
   a) A hotel in the present.
   b) A farm in high summer.
   c) A circus on a performance night.
   b) A lonely lane at night.
2. Blue main character cards:
   a) An Olympic athlete.
   b) A zoo keeper.
   c) A top chef.
   d) A fire chief.

3. Yellow essence of story line cards:
   a) A man has made a big mistake and needs time to get over it.
   b) An old person meets someone from the past and this has a huge effect on her.
   c) A person's lifelong love and work for animals is at last recognized.
   d) Someone has just come out of hospital, is glad to be alive and sees the world differently.
4. Green main object cards:
   a) A supermarket trolley.
   b) A beautiful red dress.
   c) A sealed box which contains a surprise.
   d) A garden spade.

Extended exercise to develop a KS4 focus based on this work

1. Ask students to individually write a short story based on the four elements and then get them to work in pairs and show each other their work.
2. Ask them to make suggestions for each other's story to improve and develop it. They should then redraft the stories in the light of the suggestions.

Extended exercise to develop a KS5 focus based on this work

Ask students to work in pairs. They are to write a short story based on the four elements. They are then to rewrite the story, changing one element at a time. The paired student then carefully reads the rewritten story and writes a short commentary on how the experience for the reader has changed with the alterations made.

Ask them to choose one finished story and to produce two versions, one in first person and the other in third person, narrative style. Comment on the different experiences of listening to each version.

Task 1

The four elements of the story are:

1. Setting.
2. Main character.
3. Essence of story line.
4. Main object.

Example: The dentist's waiting room

1. Setting: A dentist's waiting room.
2. Main character: Brian, a nervous patient.
3. Essence of story line: Brian becomes increasingly nervous as he waits in the waiting room and desperately thinks of an excuse to leave.
4. Main object: A huge bright orange umbrella.

Worked example of a story developed from the four elements:

The next patient came out from the dentist's room holding his cheek in much pain and Brian finally made up his mind that he was not going to stop. He would re-book his appointment! Being a coward at heart he felt that today was definitely not the day to suffer a painful filling. But what should he do? He glanced round at the other patients who were reading magazines and looking quite calm. Suddenly an idea occurred to him. He fiddled apparently casually with his huge, bright orange umbrella and 'accidentally' pressed the button which released the mechanism and the umbrella opened up.

'Oh no!' he exclaimed. He went over to the receptionist. 'I'm sorry about this, but I've done a stupid thing. My umbrella has accidentally opened indoors. I'm a terribly superstitious person and I couldn't possibly see the dentist now that this has happened. Could I, er, reappoint please – for another day?' He gave the receptionist a feeble smile.

Task 2

Setting	Main character	Essence of story line	Main object
A railway station cafe.	A disorganized man who keeps losing things has lots of bags.	He can't find his lottery ticket, but has a very strong feeling he's won. One at first, then more and more help until a crowd is helping him (thinking that they may share in his winnings).	Lottery ticket.
A trip to the zoo.	The elephant keeper who is very entertaining.	You are standing looking at the elephant when it puts out its trunk and takes your camera. The keeper has an entertaining time trying to get it back.	Your new camera.
A summertime walk in the woods.			

Task 3

Think up your own four elements and try to write a story from them.

Key skills

1. Considering unconnected things and imaginatively linking them as the basis for a piece of creative writing.

Starter

Ask students to write down thoughts which they associate with the following words:

1. Night.
2. Crew.
3. Friend.
4. Fruit.
5. Table.
6. Chest.
7. Key.
8. Island.
9. Carpenter.
10. London.

For example, 'night' might associate with: stars, darkness, moon, rest, etc.

Ask students to write an interesting sentence for each word.

Ask students to try to write a very short story (or short extract) linking together the key words. Ask them to underline each key word they use.

For example: It was now <u>night</u> and the <u>crew</u> were ready to set sail. My <u>friend</u> brought plenty of <u>fruit</u> with him to eat on the voyage. We sat at the <u>table</u> in the galley talking about our plans. There was a large wooden <u>chest</u> in the corner but the <u>key</u> was missing. We thought that a <u>carpenter</u> could take off the old lock and fit a new one. Maybe we would need a big chest to store all the things we collected once we reached the <u>island</u>. We had high hopes to return to <u>London</u> with lots of interesting stories to tell.

Main phase

Part 1

Read through, with the students, the word, phrase and sentence list in Part 1.

Ask them to try to write a short story using the words, phrases and sentences to stimulate ideas. They must use the story guide to give the story structure direction and shape.

Explain the process which they could use.

Discuss the words, phrases and sentences with their partner and plan out some ideas which might be used to link together the elements of the story. Remind them to experiment and try out different ideas. They may wish to write a rough draft version and then go through the process of editing and improvement.

Read through the example.

Part 2

Ask students to choose a list from Part 2 and Part 3 of the worksheet and then have a go themselves at writing a story using the method and style described in Part 1 above and the story guidelines.

Plenary

Students to read their stories to each other in pairs.

Suggestions for homework

Ask students to arrange to work with their parents and guardians. Parents and guardians to suggest a list of ten random things and a story line and students to write a story using that information. They then show their finished story to their parents and guardians for a comment in response.

Suggestions for development of this work

Teacher to select a classic well-known short story and select 20 key words from it. Set the students the task of writing a story based on those words using the outline plot of the classic story as a guide. Students to then read a few examples of their stories to the class and then the teacher to read the classic short story to the class, highlighting the key word when he comes to them.

Extended exercise to develop a KS4 focus based on this work

Students to work in pairs. Teacher to provide a short poem to each pair. Student 1 reads the poem (secretly) and selects ten key words from the poem. She then sets a task for her partner: she gives him the outline story line idea of the poem and the ten key words selected from that poem. The partner student is then to write a short poem using those ten key words and basing it roughly on the story outline. Partner 2 then reads his poem to partner one and partner one then reads the original poem from where the key words came. You will find that there is an intensity of concentration and appreciation of the poem after an attempt has been made to write a poem from the information provided.

Extended exercise to develop a KS5 focus based on this work

Students to carry out the exercise in KS4 Focus above and in addition write an essay to answer this question: 'Using a comparison between your own effort to write a poem and the original poem, what are the similarities and differences between the two works?'

Part 1

List 1

1. Conservatory.
2. Coach tickets.
3. Local TV.
4. Cold coffee.
5. Anonymous.
6. Bright green paper.
7. Old map.
8. Stonehenge.
9. Paint.
10. Cereal packets.

Story guide

Write a short story using the information from the list. The story has to be about something which is important but has been stolen or lost. It, however, eventually leads to good luck for the person who suffered the loss.

Story example

Danielle could not believe it. She had painstakingly spent an hour a day making her scale model of Stonehenge out of cereal packets, with bright green paper as the grass. She had painted it grey with good quality paint and had left it in the conservatory to dry. When she got home from school one day she was upset to find that it had gone missing and was nowhere to be seen. The old map of Stonehenge was gone too. That was what she had used to help her plan her scale model.

Danielle's mother was surprised that the coffee she had made for her had got cold. This was because Danielle had spent some time phoning a local TV station in the vain hope that they could appeal for its return. Interestingly the TV station did a one-minute feature on the story and invited Danielle to the studios to make her appeal.

A week went by with no news of the missing model. Then one day she received a packet through the post. It was a marvellous, professionally made model of Stonehenge and with it was a note which read:

'Dear Danielle, I saw your appeal on local TV and hope you will accept my small gift to you. I also enclose coach tickets for you and a friend to visit the real Stonehenge and make a day of it.' Anonymous.

Part 2

List 2

1. Hairstyle.
2. Waves.
3. Clever engineer.
4. Seven years
5. A successful outcome.
6. Photograph.
7. Huge advertisement.
8. Factory worker.
9. Toys.
10. Fizzy drink.

Story guide

Write a short story (or an extract of a story) using the elements on the list. The story has to be about a holiday in a hot place.

Part 3

List 3

1. Soup.
2. Person next door.
3. A waiter.
4. A chess game.
5. An empty pocket.
6. Canada.
7. Queen Victoria.
8. Swim.
9. Horse race.
10. Knitting needles.

Write a short story (or an extract of a story) using the elements on the list about meeting an important person.

Key skills

1. Writing descriptively.
2. Being able to enhance contrasts in descriptive writing.

Main phase

Part 1
Read through with students the contrasting examples in Part 1 of the worksheet and discuss with them how the whole feel of the descriptions are different. Discuss specifically how these different effects are created by considering the use of descriptive words and the distinctly different settings.

Part 2
Read through with students the list of contrasting aspects which they can use as prompts in their own writing.

Part 3
Ask students to have a go at producing two pieces of descriptive experiences which contrast pleasant and unpleasant feelings, in the style of the example. Ask students to choose their own scenarios or use the suggestion list.

Plenary

Students to read to the class examples of their work.

Suggestions for homework

Ask students to research and find two suitable contrasting pictures: one which shows a happy scene and one which shows a depressing scene. Students are then to write imaginative contrasting descriptions based on the pictures.

Suggestions for development of this work

Students to work in pairs and redraft their descriptions and suggest to each other ways in which the writing could be made more powerful and how the contrast could be made more strongly.

Extended exercise to develop a KS4 focus based on this work

Students to research and select a building they would like to live in. They then write a detailed description of the building which makes it sound wonderful. Then ask them to think for a few moments about the building falling into neglect. They then revisit the building years later. Now they write a description, as they walk round, which makes the feel of the place very unpleasant.

Extended exercise to develop a KS5 focus based on this work

Students to research and select a place they would like to visit. They then write a description of the place in detail, making it sound very pleasant, in a formal English style. They then write a description of the same place, making it sound pleasant, in a slang style. Students to then write a commentary on the differences in the language used.

Part 1

The nice experience

Holiday. Early morning, summer. A luscious slice of heaven to be hand in hand with the girl of my dreams, at last. Her dress is a light pink cotton and she seems to float through the meadow in a relaxed pace in tune with the music of the thrushes. We sit by the side of a charming burbling brook and unwrap a warm apple pie. Rabbits bound around cheerfully on the small meadows. After a few tasty mouthfuls I lean over and hand her a small white box. She opens it and smiles. The diamond reflects the beauty of the morning and sparkles a million visions of a happy future.

The unpleasant experience

Monday morning. Ten past six. November. A heavy sulphurous fog hangs heavily on the huge factory gates and I walk in automatically to my workstation. The boss looms up on me with a fiery red face and shows me a defect report from last Friday. He tuts at me and his fat bulk is threatening. Another day begins. The machines start their eternal whirling and churning and the smell of hot oil sits in the air and gets down your throat. I wander the factory floor, in and out of the grey shadows, grunting in depressed recognition of fellow workers, tightening a nut here and a bolt there. The spanner weighs heavy in my hand after all these years.

The bell for break sounds and I open my greaseproof wrapping and start eating a stale meat pie, the pastry hard on few remaining teeth. This is then washed down with tea from my flask. A tepid strong brew which leaves a taste in my mouth for the rest of the day.

Part 2

List of contrasting aspects:

1. Content and setting – where and when it is.
2. Colours.
3. Sounds.
4. Smells.
5. Taste.
6. Mood.
7. Pace and movement.
8. Person you're with.
9. Progression of events.
10. Main object.
11. Food and drink.

Part 3

Suggestion list for writing about contrasting descriptive experiences:

1. A football match: during the match compared to as the people leave.
2. A shop opening in the morning compared to closing at night.
3. A family leaving for a holiday compared with returning home early because of a problem.
4. A new puppy arrives in the family compared to a visit with it to the vets.
5. A beautiful sunny day compared to a cold, bitter, November night.

Descriptive Writing: Contrasting Places and Experiences **WORKSHEET**

Section C: Memories

Key skills

1. Writing to describe memories.

Starter

Ask students to think of objects they own which remind them of memories. Students to write about them for a few minutes.

Main phase

Part 1
Read through with the students: 'The Female Holly Blue' on the worksheet.

Part 2
Ask students to write their own account of a similar event. The suggestion list is there to help. Ask them to adopt the style of the example.

Plenary

Ask students to read to the class their own writing.

Suggestions for homework

Ask students to ask their parents and guardians if there are objects which remind them of special memories. Students can then make notes and write up the accounts in the style of the example.

Suggestions for development of this work

Compile a class folder where the various examples from the classwork and homework are collected together.

Extended exercise to develop a KS4 focus based on this work

Ask students, in timed conditions, to answer this: 'Write about a time when an object brought back memories for someone.'

Extended exercise to develop a KS5 focus based on this work

Ask students to carry out a survey and to ask a variety of teachers at the school if they would describe an object that means a lot to them because of the memories it evokes. Arrange for the spoken descriptions to be taped and then students to write out exact transcripts. With the evidence of the transcripts and with examples of written work produced from this idea, ask students to write an answer to this question: 'In what ways does a written description differ linguistically from a spoken one?'

Part 1

Imagine visiting an elderly relative. You notice something on the wall or on the mantelpiece. You ask your relative about it and they share a memory with you.

For example:

I visited my grandad the other day and I noticed a painting of a beautiful blue butterfly on the wall. The label at the foot of the painting read: 'The Female Holly Blue'.

'That's beautiful, grandad,' I said. 'Did you paint that?'

'Yes my dear boy. Yes I did.' He gave a deep sigh. 'It reminds me of . . .' He seemed to drift off somewhere in his memory.

'Yes, grandad, you were going to say . . . it reminds you of . . . please tell me.'

He looked at me with watery bright eyes. 'It reminds me of your grandmother as a matter of fact. As you know, I was happily married to that dear lady for over 50 years. It's the blue, you see. The beautiful delicate blue of the butterfly reminds me of your nanny.'

'Why is that, grandad?' I asked, intrigued.

'Well, two things really. First, she had beautiful blue eyes. They were the first thing I noticed about her when we first met.' He went off into deep thought again. 'And then I remember when we used to go butterfly spotting when we were young. We didn't have much money in those days and we had to make our own entertainments. We would chase across the meadows and then I'd hear her call: "Here's one. Here's one!" I would run over to see a beautiful butterfly. They would only be there for a few seconds and then fly off. We loved them all but our favourite was the female Holly Blue.'

Part 2

Some suggestions:

Title	Possible start of story	Further ideas – suggestions
China tea set.	'That lovely China tea set, auntie. Why do you never use it?'	Perhaps it was a gift from an old sweetheart and auntie doesn't want to use it because she wants to preserve the memory.
That old fountain pen.	'That old fountain pen, uncle. Could I have it to use at school please?' 'I'd be happy to buy you a new one my boy. But I'd prefer not to let you have that particular one.' 'Why not, uncle?' 'Well, it's a long story . . .'	Perhaps uncle used the pen years ago for a writing competition and won an important prize. Perhaps he keeps it as a lucky charm.
The cheap cow bell.	'Auntie, all the ornaments on your sideboard are antique or expensive looking. So why do you keep this little gaudy cheap cowbell?'	Maybe it was a present from a sweetheart when he brought her back a souvenir from Switzerland years ago.

The Female Holly Blue **WORKSHEET**

Key skills

1. Writing descriptively.

Starter

Ask students to list toys which they had when they were young. Ask them to make comments about what they remember about them even if the memory is foggy and faded. Even little clues will be useful.

Main phase

Part 1

Read through with the class the 'Memories of Childhood' on Part 1 of the worksheet. Point out that some things are glossed over and other things are focused on. Draw the students' attention to the useful phrases which connect the writing together to give it that sense of continuous flow. For example:

1. 'I can still see him.'
2. 'I remember seeing.'
3. 'I went to.'
4. 'We found the.'
5. 'To this day I remember.'
6. 'It's funny how little details stand out in the memory.'
7. 'But as I sit here and think, certain images take shape. For example . . .'
8. '. . . incident which stands out in my mind . . .'

Part 2

Ask students to think of a day or an incident in their early life which they remember. If they can't recall much (and they often find this bit difficult) ask them to jot down odd words and phrases from the past to see what it might trigger or spark off. Ask them to list toys they had or foods and sweets they enjoyed. That often triggers other memories.

Part 3

Ask them to write about their memories in the style of the example. Remind them that certain things might stand out and other things will be a blur. That doesn't matter, just get them to write their impressions. If there are gaps, they may wish to fill them with completely imaginative writing.

Plenary

Ask students to read their memories to their partner and vice versa.

Suggestions for homework

Ask students to chat to their parents and guardians to see if they can look through old photographs and discuss memories. They can then write a more detailed account of their memories.

Suggestions for development of this work

Arrange for students to bring in a photo of themselves when they were little, together with a short, written account of what was happening in the picture. Create a class display with the title 'Memories of Childhood'.

Extended exercise to develop a KS4 focus based on this work

Ask students to pick out a character they are currently studying in one of their selected works of literature. Ask them to write about their memories, based on the style of the example, as if they were that character. The aim is to show and explore their knowledge of the character by the way they express their memories.

Extended exercise to develop a KS5 focus based on this work

Ask students to carry out the exercise described in the KS4 Focus activity above. In addition, ask them to write the account of the childhood memories (of the chosen character) in the form of prose and then in the form of a poem.

After completing this, ask students to write an essay which answers this question: 'Does poetic language evoke the essence of memory more effectively than prose? Use your own examples to support your points.'

Memories of childhood

My special memory was when I went to France for the day on a ship which sailed from the end of the pier. It was called 'The Queen of the Channel'.

I was so excited about going on such a huge ship (it was 1964 and I was only seven) that I ran all the way and left my dad behind. I can still see him in my mind, sauntering towards the end of the pier as the ship sounded its horns!

As our ship pulled away from the coast I remember seeing a thin strip of land between sky and sea. That was my home getting smaller and smaller!

I went to the back of the ship and saw the white foam being churned up and making a track of frothy white brew on the sea which stretched back for miles.

My dad was in the bar of the ship and he let us explore wherever we wanted to. We found the engine room and to this day I remember a huge green mechanical arm rotating with a deafening noise. It's funny how little details stand out in the memory. In the joints of the rotating arm I remember the hot grease being squeezed out in little bubbles.

Many other things about the day are blurred into the memory of the past, but as I sit here and think, certain images take shape. For example, in France there was a little boy sitting in a shop doorway. He was filthy and he held out a grubby little hand for money. I remember that boy. There was a white bridge somewhere, which stretched out in dazzling sunshine which hurt my eyes. There were little bottles of cola bought for me.

The only thing I remember about the return journey was an incident which stands out in my mind very clearly. My dad had bought me a 'walking stick' which was made of plastic and was see-through and filled with thousands of tiny little multicoloured sweets. My half-brother, for a joke, tried to bend the stick and it broke, sending the sweets hurling through the air. Two things. Dad moaned at him, and he (Bob my half-brother) gave me lots of money. He was very sorry, but it's a funny thing, that to this day I still feel cheated out of those sweets!

Lastly, at the end of a busy, memorable day, we went back home and showed mum our things from France. (I wonder why my mum didn't come with us?) One of the 'things' stayed up on the wall for weeks. But each day they deflated a tiny bit until the time came for them to go in the rubbish bin. Those things were the best present any boy of seven could ever have. They were pink balloons in the shape of pigs and they had 'Calais' stamped on them and they were great. As they deflated, the printed letters of 'Calais' reduced in size until you could hardly see them.

Key skills

1. Writing to describe.
2. Writing to explain.

Starter

Ask students to write down a list of why people take photographs. After a few minutes, stop the writing activity and discuss their findings with the whole class.

Main phase

Part 1

Explain that photographs are an amazingly good way to evoke a memory. In this exercise the students are to imagine the contents of a photograph and then write an imaginary conversation between a person who knows about what is happening in the photograph and someone who is curious and asking the questions about what they see.

Read through the example in the worksheet and discuss.

Part 2

Read through the brief descriptions of the photographs and the suggestions for the conversations which could arise. Ask students to continue the conversation in writing in dialogue form in the style of the example.

Plenary

Students to read their work to each other. Ask them to discuss what images came to mind as they were being read.

Suggestions for homework

Ask students to get permission to obtain old family photographs. Ask them to interview their family members to learn what is happening in the photograph. They can then take key point notes. The next step is to write up a conversation about the contents of the photograph (with family members' permission) in the style of the example in the worksheet.

Suggestions for development of this work

Students to carry out some research on the internet or from suitable books to find and examine a variety of old photographs. They are then to find out as much as they can about the photographs. The next step is to write more informed imaginary conversations in the style of the example.

Extended exercise to develop a KS4 focus based on this work

Teacher to provide a variety of old photographs which show a variety of people and a variety of situations. They are then to select one of the characters and write a diary note in the voice of that character, describing the key events which have led up to that particular moment in time.

They can then select a scene from one of the works of literature they are studying and imagine a photograph taken at a particular moment. The next step is to describe exactly what is happening in the imaginary photograph at that particular moment in time.

Extended exercise to develop a KS5 focus based on this work

Students to carry out the exercise as described in the KS4 focus above. They then physically produce a freeze-frame of the imaginary photograph. Each student plays a character. They then explain who they are and what has led up to this point in time. A conversation can then take place between the characters about their lives and situations. The next step is to write a short essay answering this question: 'How does putting yourself into the shoes of a character in literature help you to understand that character's point of view? Use examples from the exercises you carried out in the class.'

Amy: What is this?

Arthur: A very old photograph of a classroom. That's me at the front there.

Amy: Why is everyone looking so scared, with upright backs and all holding an apple in exactly the same way?

Arthur: This was a nature study lesson. We had to handle the apple and then describe it. We all worked at exactly the same pace, as a class, step by step, doing exactly as the teacher said. If we spoke out, we would get severely punished.

Amy: Is that why you look scared?

Arthur: We look scared because we were scared. Look at the teacher standing there on his platform at the front. He dominated the classroom and everyone was scared of him.

Amy: What type of lights are those, hanging from the high ceiling?

Arthur: They are gas lights and they made a hissing sound. The light wasn't much good and if you look carefully you'll see shadows cast flickering about everywhere.

Amy: Oh yes! Those windows are so high up. How did you look out of them?

Arthur: We weren't supposed to look out of them. That would have been a distraction to our class work. Distractions were not allowed!

Amy: There's a huge open fire roaring in the hearth. Didn't you have radiators?

Arthur: No, we didn't. We had to take turns to put coal on the fire from the coal scuttle there. See it? The teacher would say: 'Smith, put some more coal on the fire!' and we had to jump to it.

Amy: Didn't he say 'Arthur'?

Arthur: No. Everything was formal and just surnames were used in those days.

Amy: What are those holes on the desks?

Arthur: They are for inkwells. We would dip our nib in and write. Paper was scarce and you were in trouble if you 'blotted your copy book' – I can tell you.

Suggested ideas to write about old photographs:

1. An old photograph showing a group of street children dressed in rags and generally very thin and scrawny playing with some stones. One of the children, who is now in her eighties, explains to her great-granddaughter how children had to make their own entertainments in the days before television.

2. An old scene showing London with horse and carriages everywhere. An old man who remembers those days explains what transport was like to a young boy.

3. A picture of a travelling fair. An old person, who used to work and travel with the fair, explains to a youngster how hard life was in those days.

4. A scene from an old farm where horses pulled the ploughs. An old retired farmer explains to a young boy what it was like to work on the farm in those days when there was little in the way of machinery.

5. An old photograph of troops setting off for war. An old war veteran explains what he can see in the picture.

What Can You See in the Photograph?   **WORKSHEET**

Key skills
1. Writing a radio play.
2. Personifying and exploring the life of objects.

Starter Activity
Ask students to write about a vivid memory they have.

Main phase
Part 1
Read through the radio play in the worksheet called 'Return journey – voices of the past'.

Discuss it with them.

Part 2
Ask them to jot down as many things as they can connected to their own memories and then try to write a radio play in the style of the example.

Plenary
Ask students in read out in role-play style the radio plays they have written.

Suggestions for homework
Ask students to find an old photograph of themselves. Use it as source material to write notes and then turn it into a short radio play in the style of the worked example.

Suggestions for development of this work
Arrange for a selection of teachers to do the exercise themselves from their own memories and arrange for them to come and read them to the students.

Extended exercise to develop a KS4 focus based on this work
Arrange for students to be able to read each other's work and write comments under the following headings:

Features of imaginative writing

1. What is the story line of the radio play?
2. Which is the most powerful character in the play, and why?
3. What mood or atmosphere is created by the writing?
4. Is there a main theme? What is it?

Extended exercise to develop a KS5 focus based on this work
Ask students to compare the radio play conversations with the four maxims of rules and conventions. For each one below, write a comment:

1. The quantity. Do the participants of the conversations say about the right amount for the purpose of their conversation?
2. Is the content relevant and appropriate to the context of the conversation?
3. Is the content delivered in a suitable manner for the purpose?
4. Is the quality of the information in the conversation suitable for the purpose?

Radio play: 'Return journey – voices of the past'

Paul has decided to visit his old primary school. He enters the main entrance.

Characters:
Paul
Polished stone floor – PSF
Small handheld blackboard – SHB
Vaulting Horse – VH
Comic book – CB

PSF:	Hello. How are you?
Paul:	Who's speaking, please?
PSF:	Look down. It's me. I'm the floor you used to walk on.
Paul:	You remembered me. How amazing.
PSF:	Yes I remember you. You were terrified the first day you came in here. Do you remember? You were five and stood shaking with fear looking down at my highly polished surface.
Paul:	I remember the smell. The smell of polish. (Lost in thought) Wait a minute, you must have had thousands of children running over your surface. How can you remember all of them?
PSF:	I don't remember all of them. (Pause) But I remember you. Go on, go into Classroom 3 and see if anyone in there remembers you.
Narrator:	Paul walks slowly from the corridor to Classroom 3. He opens the door and walks in.
SHB:	Come on. Don't be shy. Come and feel what I'm like to hold, now you're all grown up. There are some different coloured chalks in that jar.
Paul:	But I thought schools would have laptops and things now?
SHB:	They do. They're all over there, look. But the headteacher likes tradition, thank goodness. That's why we've been kept in this special display cabinet. Come on, pick me up.
Paul:	Are you the actual one I wrote on?
SHB:	I can even tell you the colour of the chalk you chose. It was purple.
Paul:	Yes, that's right.
Narrator:	Paul selects a piece of purple chalk.
SHB:	Go on, see if you can remember the first thing you wrote on me. I was brand-new then.
Paul:	It was my name.
SHB:	That's it. Go on then, write it. (There is the screeching sound of chalk) Pop into the Gym while you're here. They'd love to see you.
Narrator:	Paul walks back into the corridor and down to the Gym. (There is the sound of the Gym door opening)
VH:	I know you never liked me, did you?
Paul:	I was scared of you.
VH:	You should have overcome your fear. It's never too late. Come on, vault over me now.
Narrator:	Paul removes his jacket and takes a run at it and leaps over it easily.
VH:	See, easy.
Paul:	Well it is now, because you're so small.
VH:	See, I knew you didn't like me. You're insulting me now. I don't suppose you ever became a great sportsman?
Paul:	You're right about that. It's because of you. You scared me when I was very little.
VH:	Oh get out of here and leave me in peace. I didn't like you then and I don't like you now. Go away.
Narrator:	Paul hesitates, gives a big sigh and leaves. He wanders down to the library and opens the door.
CB:	You're back! Come here. Come on, quickly.
Paul:	Hello, how are you?
CB:	Not so good these days. I'm always left alone mainly. With all the computer games and stuff, nobody much bothers with good old-fashioned comic books like me any more.
Paul:	Well, let me have a look. (He flicks through the comic pages, stopping here and there) I loved you. I used to sit in here for hours reading you. It was a great escape.
CB:	Escape? From what.
Paul:	From school dinners. Do you remember, I used to hate them?
CB:	That's right. You used to sit huddled in that corner and eat your sandwiches, over me, didn't you?
Paul:	Yes.
CB:	You used to drop crumbs that got stuck between my pages. But never mind. I wish someone would read me now with the interest you used to show me.

Return Journey   **WORKSHEET**

Key skills

Writing dramatic monologues of people's memories.

Starter

Ask students to list things that stand out in their memories. Can they explain why certain things stand out?

For example, the time they fell off their bike.

Main phase

Part 1

Read through with students 'The usherette' in Part 1 of the worksheet. Point out that a dramatic monologue is spoken by one person and includes the following features:

1. A silent audience.
2. Reference to the reactions of the listener: for example, 'I see you smile at that; well, let me explain.'
3. An unfolding of that character's thoughts and feelings, revealing a lot about the character and past events.

Part 2

Ask students to choose from the suggestion list in Part 2 of the worksheet and write a dramatic monologue in the style of the example in Part 1 of the worksheet.

Plenary

Students to read to each other, in pairs, their dramatic monologues.

Suggestions for homework

Ask students to research about jobs from the past. They then select one and put themselves in the 'shoes' of an elderly person who can recall key memories about that particular job. They then write a dramatic monologue in the style of the example in Part 1 of the worksheet, for that character.

Suggestions for development of this work

Arrange for students to interview members of their own families and take notes about key memories which stand out for them. They then create dramatic monologues based on those notes. The next stage is to rehearse readings of the monologues and as a group suggest to each other improvements and refinements. The objective is to make the monologues as interesting and entertaining for the listener as possible. The final stage is to arrange for a presentation of the readings of the monologues to the whole class.

Extended exercise to develop a KS4 focus based on this work

Ask students to think of someone they admire. They are then to find out as much as possible about that person and from that information write a dramatic monologue, as if they were that person, focusing on memories which stand out.

Extended exercise to develop a KS5 focus based on this work

Ask students to select a character from one of the works of literature which they are currently studying. The next stage is to write a dramatic monologue, as if they were that character, recalling events from their life and showing, at the same time, accurate knowledge of the story. They then write an essay, in response to this work, answering this question: 'How does a dramatic monologue help us to understand a character in a work of fiction? Give specific examples from your own work in this area.'

Part 1

The usherette

What's that you say? What stands out in my memory? Is that what you're asking? Well now. Let me think for a few moments about that. Well, when I was young I used to work as an usherette in a cinema. I can see by the look on your face that you're confused. Well, an usherette had to show people to their seats in the cinema, you see. There was a strict code of conduct in those days. I'm going back years, you know. I had to stand to attention when the customers arrived. We usherettes all had to wear smart uniforms. I then had to shine a faint blue beam, from a torch, onto the floor and take customers quietly to their seats, so as not to disturb the other customers. There was quite a skill, quite a knack to it, I can tell you. I can see by your expression that you don't think that is much fun. But it was. We got to see all the latest films and I got to know the names of every actor and actress by watching the credits roll up at the end. When you'd seen them 50 times you remembered them, I can tell you. There was something else too. Some of the 'well to dos' used to give us a few shillings as a tip. And there was one other thing. If a boy came in and I fancied him I could ask him for a date as he walked out. One thing that sticks in my memory is when Mr Boston, the manager, told me off for talking to a boy while on duty. 'If you do that again,' he said with a rather fierce face, 'you won't have a job here any more.' That made the whole thing a bit of a game. It was great fun trying to chat to the boys and not get caught by old grumpy-pants! I can see you laughing there, but that is what we called him: old grumpy-pants! Those were the days . . .

Part 2

Suggestions to write dramatic monologues about:

1. Someone who worked in a factory years ago. Perhaps what stands out is the contrast between the pain of the awful monotony of the job and the pleasure of making great workmates.
2. Someone who used to model clothes. Maybe they got to meet some really interesting people.
3. A gardener who used to work at Buckingham Palace. Maybe she remembers the day the Queen came over to compliment her flowers.
4. Someone who used to sell ice cream on the beach in the summer. Maybe he remembers what great fun it was to be paid for being out in the sunshine.
5. A television camera operator. Maybe she remembers meeting some famous people.

What Stands Out in Your Memory? **WORKSHEET**

Section D: Something Special

Key skills

1. Writing to explain and describe in detail.

Starter

Ask students to write down something they would love to be able to create if time and money were not an issue.

Main phase

Part 1

Read through Part 1 of the worksheet with students which shows the stages of the creation of an example 'masterpiece'.

Part 2

Read through with students and ask them to have a go at writing their own 'masterpiece' using the step-by-step approach.

Plenary

Ask students to read out examples of their work to the class.

Suggestions for homework

Ask students to ask their parents or guardians what their dreams of a 'masterpiece' are. Students to make detailed notes and write out in detail using the step-by-step approach. Students to ask parents or guardians to read the finished product and write a comment.

Suggestions for development of this work

Everyone has dreams. Arrange for students to interview members of staff and ask them what their dreams are. Students to make detailed notes and write out in detail using the step-by-step approach. Teachers to write comments on the finished product.

Extended exercise to develop a KS4 focus based on this work

Students to work in pairs and present a spoken presentation to the rest of the class, explaining more details about their plans and ideas and taking a question-and-answer session.

Extended exercise to develop a KS5 focus based on this work

Students to follow through the exercises on the worksheet and produce a fully written out 'masterpiece'. Imagine that the press are impressed by the 'masterpiece' and run an article on it. Students to produce suitable articles for tabloid and broadsheet papers. They then write commentaries which will outline the linguistic features used.

Part 1

Imagine that you have gone to a lot of time and trouble to create a 'masterpiece'.

Think about the stages which you have gone through.

First step: your interest and desire to create something special.

Second step: the plan of action.

Third step: the creation itself.

Fourth step: the admiration stage, using it and showing it off and seeing the reactions from others.

Look at the worked example.

The creation of an abstract painting

Step 1: Interest and desire to create something special

I love art and have wanted, for years, to create an abstract painting. Not any old abstract painting. An abstract painting which I could take to a London gallery and see what they thought of it. The problem was, I kept putting it off and never seemed to get round to doing it.

Step 2: Plan of action

I knew I would need some resources. A large piece of canvas and some oil paints and brushes. Some pencil sketches, photographs and some time to do it. I decided to set myself one hour a week on a Sunday afternoon from 4 pm until 5 pm for ten weeks. I wrote down the dates on a sheet of paper entitled: 'The action plan for a masterpiece'. I even wrote a date by which I would save up the money required to buy the materials and the train fare to London, etc. I figured that if I saved £5 per week for 20 weeks I would have £100. The canvas and paints would be £40 and the rest would be the trip to London. I researched to find the appropriate art galleries and sent letters to try to make an appointment (I gave several possible dates and times). I realized that I would have to write many letters and ask many times before someone would agree to see it. I eventually got a nice letter back showing an interest and arranging a ten-minute slot with an art dealer on a particular date. Isn't that interesting! He agreed to see my painting and it wasn't created yet. That is the beauty of planning!

Step 3: The creation

I had had an idea to paint a picture of my dad's old bakery. An abstract painting messes the images up but I thought that would make it interesting. I went and visited the old bakery and found it to be in a state of disrepair. I took lots of pictures and when I got back to my 'studio' I started to sketch out various images. I also used reference pictures of bakery machinery and an old coal-fired oven.

Step 4: The admiration stage, using it and showing it off and seeing the reactions from others

The day arrived and I proudly set off for the big city with a friend of mine. We were very well treated by the gallery and one of the art experts gave his opinion. They were kind enough to display it to the public for three hours. A book of comments was placed by the exhibit and I now have a dozen or so interesting opinions of my work.

The plan was a great success and I'm pleased I took the time and trouble to do it. I feel I've achieved something special.

Part 2

Your turn.

Following the steps above, have a go at writing out in detail your own 'masterpiece'. Your 'masterpiece' can be anything which is your dream and desire. The important thing is to visualize and write out in detail following the four steps. The creative thinking part is 'How can I get from where I am to where I want to go?', and then write out the steps.

Suggestions to choose from:

1. Singing with a famous pop group.
2. Performing in a circus.
3. Meeting a famous astronaut.

Creating Your 'Masterpiece' **WORKSHEET**

'The film of familiarity which blinds us all from the wonder of our being' (Wordsworth)

Key skills

1. Developing powers of observation.
2. Writing to describe in very close detail.

Starter activity

Ask students to write down a list of ten everyday activities which are repeated every day almost without thinking. For example: tying up shoelaces; opening a letter received in the post . . .

Main phase

Part 1

1. Explain that when things are familiar to us we don't really look at them carefully. In this activity we are going to take a fresh look at familiar activities and notice little details.
2. Read with the class 'Boiling an Egg' on the worksheet.

Part 2

Ask them to do the task in Part 2. Remind them to try to imagine in detail, paying particular attention to colours, shapes and movement. Remind them to look out for something in the process which might imaginatively resemble something else. Use a simile if it will help bring the description alive.

Part 3

Read through with the students Part 3 on the worksheet, where a familiar process is slowed right down. A good way to illustrate this is to carry out a process in the classroom and get the students to observe and comment. Stop the process at key points. For example, tying a tie.

Part 4

Ask students to do the activity in Part 4.

Plenary

Students to hear a few good examples of descriptions read out in the class. Explain that the activity will help when it comes to bringing descriptive writing alive by using details.

Suggestions for homework

Students to look out for a familiar routine process at home and write about it using the methods learned in the class today. This will reinforce the process of noticing details.

Suggestions for development of this work

Create a class wall display called 'The Extraordinary Hidden Within the Ordinary'. Choose a process from the best examples produced by the class and arrange for students to produce illustrations which can be clearly labelled with the detailed descriptions using arrows and so on.

Extended exercise to develop a KS4 focus based on this work

Ask students to examine an object very closely and describe it in great detail.

Extended exercise to develop a KS5 focus based on this work

1. Ask students to research an antique of their choice and to produce a detailed description of it using the formal style suitable for an entry into an auction catalogue.
2. Ask students to prepare a role play based on the same antique as mentioned in '1' above. Students are to write out the words of a role play which would show a scene where an antique dealer attempts to sell the antique to a customer using informal spoken language.
3. Students to write a report comparing the written version with the spoken transcript and identify similarities and differences in the language.

Part 1

Boiling an egg

Imagine an egg in a saucepan of gently simmering water. Look carefully. What do you see? The little bubbles of the boiling water have a silvery colour to them. They seem to scramble around the smooth shape of the egg, and then rush to the surface of the water. What do the bubbles resemble? Perhaps they are the eggs of aliens. As they hit the surface of the water they burst and the contents vanish in a blink of the eye.

Part 2

Look at the list of everyday small events. Pick one of them and try to describe it in a detailed way, using the style of the example above.

1. Putting on a wrist watch.
2. Tying a shoe lace.
3. Drying your hair.
4. Brushing your teeth.

Try to think of further everyday small events and describe them in a detailed way.

Part 3

Imagine the process of an everyday event being slowed right down so that you have time to notice little things. For example, making a cup of tea could be broken down into stages:

1. Look inside the cup and notice the reflected light and shadow on the smooth white surface.
2. Drop in the teabag and listen for the faint sound as it hits the inside of the cup.
3. The boiling water is carefully poured in and the teabag changes from white to brown. The steam engulfs the cup like a tiny mist.
4. You stir the bag and notice the water change colour to black. A little milk is poured in and the colour changes to cloudy white and then suddenly a rich brown. Particularly notice how the milk mixes with the water.
5. You stir the liquid and see the eddy pools circling and bubbles appear. The centre of the surface of the liquid dips down a little.

Part 4

Now imagine your own familiar everyday small event and describe it in a similar way where the component parts are slowed right down and described in great detail.

The Extraordinary Hidden Within the Ordinary   **WORKSHEET**

Key skills

1. Experimenting with the writing of poems.

Starter

Ask students to discuss and then list times when a poem would be read.

Main phase

Part 1

Read through with the class the task and the example poem. Ask them to choose one of the suggestions for them to write a poem in the same form as the example.

Point out to them the rhyming pattern of ABAB.

Part 2

Read through with the class the task and the example poem. Ask them to choose one of the suggestions for them to write their own poem in a similar form to the example.

Part 3

Read through with the class the task and the example poem. Ask them to choose one of the suggestions for them to write their own poem in a similar form to the example.

Plenary

Students to read their poems to each other and discuss which parts they particularly liked, and why.

Suggestions for homework

Ask students to think of an important time in their life and try to write a short poem about it in the style of the examples worked on in the class.

Suggestions for development of this work

Arrange to have the poems produced from the homework assembled into a class poetry book. Students may like the idea of illustrating each other's poems.

Extended exercise to develop a KS4 focus based on this work

Students to be given a week or more to research and collect as many different types of poems and to find out what they are called (the style and form). They can then be kept in an indexed class folder to refer to when doing poetry work.

Extended exercise to develop a KS5 focus based on this work

Students to carry out the task described in the KS4 Focus and in addition to annotate the poems with as many technical terms as they can identify.

Part 1

Task: Imagine you come across an ancient lane in the countryside which seems to wind into the distance and then disappear. It looks intriguing, and you wonder about the history of the travellers of the past who have taken this route. You want to write a short poem about your thoughts and feelings. Perhaps it might go something like this:

Lane
Look at this lane, where does it go?
Winding to a mysterious place.
No one can say that they really know,
About the travellers of old, gone without trace.

Suggestions:

1. Imagine that it is a fine bright morning and you are in a busy city. You start to think about all the travelling, movement and energy around you: the birds flying; a plane high in the sky; a bus going by; bicycles; people walking; cars and vans . . . everything seems to be moving. Write a poem to suggest the energy and movement of the city.
2. Imagine that you are in a museum of natural history. You become fascinated by the fossils which are images of life from millions of years ago. Write a poem about them.
3. Imagine you are on holiday in Spain. It is evening and you are walking on the prom by the beach. Artists have produced dozens of fantastically intricate sand sculptures of everything from angels to monsters complete with tiny details. You admire them and think they are great. Then you realize that overnight the sea will come in and wash them all away. Write a poem about your thoughts and feelings.

Part 2

Task: Imagine that you are a tourist and you see a donkey which has been loaded up with various materials to carry. You feel sorry for the donkey, particularly the way it just seems to serve and not complain. You write out your feelings in a short poem. Perhaps something like this:

Loaded donkey

There's not an animal I know
As loyal as this one is;
Standing patiently in the sun
Serving people with no reward
Except the occasional bun.

Suggestions:

1. Imagine that you are on holiday and see an elephant at work, moving huge logs with its powerful trunk. You are struck by the power and slow confident movement of the giant creature. Write a short poem about it.
2. Imagine you are at a museum and you are looking at a life-size, wonderfully detailed and realistic model of a sabre-toothed tiger. You imagine what it must have been like when it roamed this earth. You feel the fear of the sight of it. Write a poem to explain your fear.
3. Imagine you get the chance to experience a real thrill. You go diving in the ocean in a special cage which protects you from, but also allows you to experience close up, full-size sharks in their natural environment. You find the experience truly awesome as they charge at you and then change direction at the last moment. Write a poem about the thrill of it.

Part 3

Task: Imagine that you have been travelling on a ship at sea. You have come to respect the power of the sea and want to write a poem to express your feelings. Perhaps it might be like this:

The sea

The waves and foam and swirling mass
I've travelled on some time;
I realize that the core of its power
Is far greater than mine.

Suggestions:

1. Imagine that you are flying for the first time. You feel overwhelmed by the experience. Write a short poem about your thoughts and feelings.
2. Imagine that you look up at a clear night sky and suddenly realize the immensity of the universe, and at the same time, how tiny you are. Write a poem about how you feel.
3. Imagine you are walking with friends on a hot summer's day in the countryside. You suddenly become overwhelmed by a feeling of deep joy. Write a poem to express how you feel.

Poetic Considerations **WORKSHEET**

Key skills

1. Using persuader words.
2. Descriptive writing.

Starter

Ask students to imagine that they want to sell something they own. Ask them to write an advert for it using as many persuader words as they can.

Main phase

Part 1

Read through with your students the piece called 'Fruit Advert'. Ask them to say what images came into their minds when they listened. The words of the description of the advert create a framework of images in the mind into which the listener's imagination adds the details and fills the gaps.

Part 2

Read through with them the piece called 'The lawn mower'. Again, ask them to discuss the images which came to mind.

Draw attention to the positive and inviting images which are used.

Part 3

Discuss with students the 'Advert suggestion list – brief details' and ask them to describe an advert in words, in the style of the examples. They may wish to use the suggestion list or they can design entirely their own advert, using only words. The important thing is to describe it in such a way that the listener can picture the actual advert in their mind's eye.

Plenary

Students to work in pairs. One student to read his advert and his partner to do a quick sketch in response.

Suggestions for homework

Ask students to find an advert in a magazine and write a detailed description of it. Ask them also to extract the persuader words and phrases (and images).

Suggestions for development of this work

Students to study in groups a collection of adverts from magazines and work out commonly reoccurring features. They can then produce a chart to display their findings with particular emphasis on techniques of persuasion used.

Extended exercise to develop a KS4 focus based on this work

Students to find a TV advert which they like and write an answer to this question: 'How does the advert persuade you to buy the product or service?'

Extended exercise to develop a KS5 focus based on this work

Students to find a TV advert which they like and write an answer to this question: 'How does the advert persuade you to buy the product or service? Write a detailed commentary including examples.'

Part 1

Fruit advert

Look at those lovely slices of succulent pink melons. They are right at the front of the advert and we can see the details of the juice sparkling in tropical light. Notice how your eye is smoothly drawn into the middle ground where we see a pale yellow beach stretching in a smooth curve by a blue, blue sea. The beach is over-arched by swaying palm trees bathed in golden light. The holidaymakers run on the beach and swim in the sea, smiling with the joy of life! Our eye makes its way to the background of the advert's scene, where a delightful grey and pale purple mountain range borders the deep blue sky. Your eye returns once more to the melons, and the juice and the anticipation of the sweet, cool, tasting experience. Above the advert, the words read: 'The Famous Fruit Company. Fruit from Paradise.'

Part 2

The lawn mower

Look at that huge green lawn. From the hedged edges to the edge of the house it lies there, mown perfectly with crisscross geometric patterns of light and darker green. Look at the woman. She has finished her mowing and now enjoys a cup of tea, sitting relaxed on the garden bench. She wears blue jeans and a fresh white shirt. Her eyes sweep across the vista of flat lawn and she looks very pleased with herself. You can smell the newly mown grass. And there, by her side, sits the proud lawnmower. It has done its work. It seems to be saying: 'That was effortless. Give me another lawn to do . . .' The words above the advert read: 'Regatta Lawnmowers. Because your lawn deserves the best.'

Advertisements **WORKSHEET**

Key skills

1. Writing to describe.
2. Imagining and writing about unusual attractions.

Starter

Ask students to think of five well-known businesses and why it is attractive to be a customer of theirs.

Main phase

Part 1

Read through with students the example of the Balmoral Restaurant.

Part 2

Ask students to try to write about a business which has a special feature to attract customers. Students may wish to use the suggestion box to give them ideas.

Plenary

Students to read out their ideas to the class.

Suggestions for homework

Ask students to pick an idea which they haven't worked on yet from the suggestion box in Part 2 on the worksheet. They can then spend more time writing out another idea more fully with more details.

Suggestions for development of this work

Students to review one of their special feature business ideas and design and produce a poster advert using persuasive language to advertise the service.

Extended exercise to develop a KS4 focus based on this work

Ask students to imagine that the local press have picked up on your special feature business idea. They intend to write a news article about the unusual service. Students to write that article in the style of a newspaper.

Extended exercise to develop a KS5 focus based on this work

Ask students to imagine that the local press have become interested in the special feature you are using in your business. They intend to write a news article about the unique and unusual service. Students are then to write that article in newspaper style. Then, alongside the article, a full-page advert is to be placed. Students to design and produce that advert and then write a commentary which explains how the language of the advert persuades readers to become interested in the service offered.

The Balmoral Restaurant

The food was basic, not at all exciting. The décor was faded yellows and greens. The service was friendly enough but perhaps a little slow. The Balmoral Restaurant could only really be called 'mediocre'. So why was it that on a Friday morning so many customers queued up to come in? The reason was simple. It was Sharon.

Sharon was an art student who had made an agreement with the restaurant owner to sit and draw the customers' portraits. She would sit there in her multi-coloured patchwork dress working furiously with her pencils. Very often there would be a snap as the pencils broke under the power of her artistic enthusiasm.

She would talk all the way through, and often in an embarrassing way. Things like: 'Big ears, hair tufting out, long nose, quite ugly . . . .horrible wrinkles . . . big fat cheeks . . . red face . . . etc.'. But the customers didn't mind because they would, in the end, be presented with a brilliant sketch which captured the essence of who they were. Very often a customer would just stand and stare at the finished work of art. It was not unusual for a tear to appear in a customer's eye.

The restaurant owner Gregory would ask if Sharon could come more often, but Friday was the only day she could be sure of with her busy schedule. In payment, Sharon was offered all the food she could eat. She re-negotiated the deal to cash payments. Gregory, with all his extra customers, was always in profit. You see, as a customer, to qualify for a free portrait you had to order a meal.

Choose from the suggestion box below:

Place of business	Person with special skill (Character key points)	What is the special skill?	Opening sentence and ideas and suggestions
1. Restaurant: The Balmoral Restaurant.	Sharon the artist with crazy clothes.	Fast sketch which captures the likeness brilliantly.	'The food was basic, not at all exciting. The décor was faded yellows and greens.'
2. A shoe repair shop: 'Beatrice Repairs Souls!'.	Beatrice.	Sings a song while customers wait.	Not all the customers were happy with the arrangement.
3. The coal office: 'Fulton's Coal'.	Charlie.	Reads palms and tells fortunes.	As coal offices go, Fulton's was quite a boring place to be in. Boring, that is, apart from an old bloke called Charlie.
4. Tyre and exhaust garage.	Bob.	Retired circus clown.	Some people loved 'Budget Exhausts' in the High Street. Others would not go there under any circumstances. The reason was nothing to do with the service. The thing that divided customers was Bob.
5. The flower shop: 'Petals'.	Titania.	An acrobat.	When you order a bunch of red roses you don't expect someone in a flowing green costume to bring them to you doing cartwheels! But in Petals the flower shop that is what you can expect!

The Special Feature **WORKSHEET**

Key skills

1. Writing a mini play.
2. Imagining inventions.

Starter activity

Ask students to write down ten inventions.

Teacher tip: You could start off with a class discussion where you as the teacher suggest a few to get the discussion and ideas going. For example: telephone; radio; television; bicycle; car; computer; book . . .

Main phase

Part 1

1. Setting the scene in the minds of the students.
   Explain that today we are going to imagine what it is like to invent something new and experience the circumstances which could follow on from an invention.
2. Read the mini play, on the worksheet, to the class, with you reading one part and a student reading the other.
3. Ask the students to write down what types of thing could go wrong in the first few months of production.
4. Ask students to imagine that a year has passed and the sales have been fantastic. Write out a short mini play in the style of the example where the investor is overjoyed with how things have gone.

Part 2

Read through with the class the alternative scenario on the worksheet. Ask students to write the mini play using the starter example if they wish to and then continue.

Plenary

Arrange for a few of the mini scripts to be read out to the class.

Suggestions for homework

Ask students to research and list five important inventions in history. Can they explain the importance of each one in their own words?

Suggestions for development of this work

Ask students to research an important invention in history. Imagine they were the inventor. Write a letter to a friend, as if they were the inventor, explaining the invention and how it works.

Extended exercise to develop a KS4 focus based on this work

Students to work in pairs and write out, in detail, a mini play where an inventor in history explains his invention to a member of the public.

Extended exercise to develop a KS5 focus based on this work

Ask students to thoroughly research an invention and present an information leaflet which explains in detail how the invention works. Students should also write a commentary on how they put the leaflet together and what the language considerations were.

Part 1
The invention

Introduction

An inventor has invented an exciting new product and is trying to explain to an investor the difficulties he has been through to get to this point. He needs the investment of £10,000 in order to start production of the product. If the product sells and does well, both inventor and investor will be rich. If it flops, a lot of time money and energy will be lost. A great deal of disappointment will follow.

A = The inventor
B = The investor

B   Could I first of all ask what it is?

A   Certainly. (Big smile) You are looking at the world's first voice-change tablet set.

B   Could you explain?

A   Certainly. You will notice that the tablets are in ten colours in this little convenient packet.
The key for the colours is on the back of the packet. You see, for example, that blue means strong, deep voice, whereas yellow means sharp, high-pitched voice. You simply chew the tablet and within one minute your voice changes to the desired dream voice and this will last for up to ten hours.

B   Amazing! How on earth did you do it?

A   Well, I was good at chemistry at school and one day, while I was mixing up all sorts of chemicals and compounds at home, I accidentally picked up a beaker of some strange mixture, and thinking that it was my tea, I drunk it down and ended up sounding like Elvis Presley! After a few hours the effect wore off.

B   Then what did you do?

A   Well, I tried endless experiments, mainly on myself, and found that the compounds I was using could alter the vocal harmony of the voice box.

B   And you need me to invest £10,000 for the commercial production of these tablets? Who will they sell to?

A   Just imagine it. Actors, salespeople, television presenters, partygoers . . . the possibilities are endless.

B   And there are no side effects?

A   None whatsoever! I've been experimenting on myself for years and I've experienced no ill effects at all.

B   What will the money be for?

A   Basically, to protect my idea I must patent it. Then I need to buy raw materials and rent a laboratory and start the manufacturing process. Then there'll be the costs of advertising and transporting it to the shops. But my dream is that within hardly any time we'll be millionaires!

B   You've convinced me. The money is yours. Cheque or cash?

Part 2

Now imagine an alternative scenario.

Read this extract to the class taken from a letter from the inventor to the investor:

'I have now developed a new idea for combining the tablets so that virtually any celebrity voice can be achieved. For example, one-half of blue plus two browns and one-quarter white gives you exactly the Prime Minister's voice.'

The new tablets sell incredibly well but a huge problem looms up. Once taken, the voice does not change back to normal in ten hours but stays as the person's permanent voice!

Write out a mini play exploring the scenario where the inventor agrees to meet with several angry customers for a news conference. Students may wish to use the following as a start to the mini play and then develop it themselves:

A = Inventor
B = Angry customer 1
C = Angry customer 2
D = Angry customer 3

A: First of all, may I apologise for the mistake. I've been up all night worrying about it.

B: It's all right for you, but I've got to sound like Sir Winston Churchill for the rest of my life!

A: It is a nice voice.

B: (Getting angry) I don't care, I want my old voice back.

The Invention   **WORKSHEET**

Key skills

1. Writing to advise.
2. Writing a mini radio play.

Starter

Ask students to write an answer to this question: 'What is the best advice that you have ever been given?'

Main phase

Part 1

Read with the class the radio play in Part 1 called: 'Always in a hurry'. The teacher can be grandad and a student can read Freddie.

Part 2

Read through the suggestion list with the students and discuss. Ask them to choose one and write a mini radio play in the style of the example.

Plenary

Arrange for students to read out, in pairs, the mini plays to the rest of the class.

Suggestions for homework

Ask students to ask their parents and guardians about good general advice about life which they've been given, perhaps a while ago, and have valued. Students to write it out and share with the class next lesson.

Suggestions for development of this work

Arrange for students to edit and redraft their mini radio plays and expand them and record them and add sound-effects to make it a realistic radio play.

Extended exercise to develop a KS4 focus based on this work

Students to produce clearly written, neatly presented advice leaflets for teenagers covering a range of topical issues.

Extended exercise to develop a KS5 focus based on this work

Students to collate a variey of sources of advice writing. They are to then write an essay on this question: 'What are the main features of advice in its written form?' They can illustrate the essays with examples of well-written advice from their sources.

Part 1

A radio play called 'Always in a hurry'

Grandad: Freddie, would you sit down a moment, I want to have a word with you.

Freddie: I'll have to look sharp, grandad, I'm meeting my friends in five minutes.

Grandad: Come on, calm down a bit, you look like you're in a dreadful hurry.

Freddie: (Glancing at his huge wrist watch) Yes, I'm running a bit late. Shall we chat tomorrow?

Grandad: Actually, it was the subject of being in a rush which I wanted to talk to you about.

Freddie: What do you mean? (Sounding rather puzzled and surprised)

Grandad: It's just that I've noticed that you're always in a hurry. You get up, hurry your breakfast. You hurry off to school, you always leave late. I bet you hurry through the day, don't you? And then, I hear the door go when you get home, and before you can look round you've chucked your school clothes everywhere and you're off again, like a shot.

Freddie: Everyone hurries, grandad.

Grandad: Let me tell you something, Freddie. When I was your age I couldn't wait to leave school and get a job. As you know, I got a job at the dock and I couldn't wait to get promoted. Then I couldn't wait to get married, then I couldn't wait to have children. I was always in a hurry you see. I couldn't wait to earn more money and buy a bigger house. Before I could look round I was counting my days to my pension. I couldn't wait to get money every month and not have to work any more. I thought I'd be able to do all the things I'd always wanted to do.

Freddie: And did you, grandad?

Grandad: (Long pause, then with a thoughtful, sad voice) . . . I was sitting here this afternoon thinking. (Pause) Freddie, I wish I hadn't hurried so much. (Pause and deep sigh) It becomes a sort of habit, you see. You never enjoy the moment. You're always hurrying along to the next thing.

Freddie: What do you mean, 'You never enjoy the moment'?

Grandad: Just that, Freddie. You see, this afternoon I was looking out of the window at some sparrows washing themselves in the birdbath. The sun was glistening on their feathers. It was just nice to watch, that's all. There was no need to hurry, I just . . . I just enjoyed watching them. I suppose what I mean is I was enjoying the feeling of being alive.

Freddie: So you want me to stop hurrying?

Grandad: All I'm saying, Freddie, is that if I could be your age again, which I know I can't, but if I could, I would make it a habit of mine to slow down and notice what's around me more and, enjoy the moment. (Long pause) You see, life is made up of millions of little ordinary moments and, well, we should slow down for a while and, well, notice them. (Long pause). Anyway, enough of me, I suppose you'd better see your friends, hadn't you?

Freddie: I've changed my mind, grandad. (Pause) I think I'll stay here and watch the birds in the birdbath . . .

Part 2

Situations where advice could be offered:

1. Reformed criminal offering advice to a young offender.
2. Someone who was a slow learner at school but was able, with extra hard work, to catch up and overtake and eventually become a teacher, to a student who is struggling with her work and getting downhearted about it.
3. A person who is filled with enthusiasm for life giving advice to someone who is bored with everything.
4. Someone who has a lot of friends offering advice to someone who finds it hard to make friends.
5. Someone who has been careful with money offering advice to someone who has squandered their money.

The Advice **WORKSHEET**

49

Section E: Spooky Business

Key skills

1. Writing a short story.
2. Introducing tension and atmosphere.

Starter

Ask students to write briefly about a time when they got lost. Where were they and how did they feel? Spend about ten minutes on this.

Main phase

Part 1

Read the story in the worksheet with the students. Discuss how atmosphere and mood are created.

Part 2

Ask students to discuss and jot down notes about how the story may continue.

Part 3

Ask students to write their own story about an imaginative experience where they got lost. This can be made up or real.

Plenary

A couple of students to read their stories to the class.

Suggestions for homework

Ask students to find a picture which has a spooky atmosphere. Ask them to write a story, inspired by the picture, about someone being lost.

Suggestions for development of this work

Obtain a copy of *The Hound of the Baskervilles* by Sir Arthur Conan Doyle. Divide it up and sequence it so that each student has a small section. Organize for them to take their section home and have a chance to study it and look out for particular places which create a spooky mood and atmosphere. Arrange a session where the students read the whole story in sequence. It works well if the story is abridged and the teacher reads the linking passages to keep the momentum going.

Extended exercise to develop a KS4 focus based on this work

Students to compile an information sheet detailing of aspects of writing, drawn from examples of great literature, where a spooky atmosphere is created. Small examples can be copied on to support the information. A couple of good examples would be:

1. The journey across the moor when Dr Watson first visited Baskerville Hall in *The Hound of the Baskervilles* by Sir Arthur Conan Doyle.
2. Act 1 Scene 1 in *Hamlet* by William Shakespeare.

Extended exercise to develop a KS4 focus based on this work

Students to rewrite 'The Tavern' in first-person narrative and then compare it to the third person. Write an answer to this question: 'How does the experience of the reader change with the change of narrative structure?'

'Douglas Rathbone requests the pleasure of your company to celebrate his sixtieth birthday party at the Bearded Sailor, North Wharf, Greystone Quay, Iptown. Seven until late.'

Charles read the card again in the flickering light of his lighter. He had been driving around now in the pouring rain for nearly an hour. The place was deserted. There was no one to ask directions and most of the derelict road signs were so badly deteriorated that deciphering them was impossible, especially in such gloomy light. The occasional streetlamp was working but it gave merely a faint yellow glow. Road after road of deserted warehouses loomed up as dark shapes everywhere, and Charles, normally persistent by nature, was on the cusp of giving up. As he read the gold embossed words again, he thought he would have one last try. So he set off again, intending to explore the area down the road a bit where he vaguely felt he might have more luck. His mind continued to attempt to bring up the image of the face of Douglas Rathbone. The name was familiar in his very early past, but he just couldn't think of his face now.

As he glanced to the left down a side road, at one point he thought he caught a glimpse of a window with a light behind it. He stopped his car and reversed. He headed for the window. The route took him down a very narrow and sinister-looking alley, just wide enough for the car. In the distance was indeed a faint light and as he drew closer he saw a dark, rather large figure on the corner of the next junction. He pulled his car up and wound down the window.

'Excuse me sir, can you tell me where the tavern called "The Bearded Sailor" is?' The figure lurched towards the vehicle and thrust his head into the interior. Charles found himself face to face with a huge, ginger-bearded head, dripping with rain, whose rugged features told immediately of a life of hardship and bad luck. Charles smelt rum and strong pipe tobacco.

'You ain't far, as it happens. You're just there, look!' He swung a massive arm towards the faint orange light ahead.

'Thank you. I've been invited to a party there,' said Charles, wary of this odd, lonely figure pressing himself so far into his car, and at the same time relieved he had found the tavern at last.

'Party in there! You'll be lucky!' came the surprising reply. He pulled himself out of the car and started to shuffle off in the opposite direction. He was laughing out loud and repeating, 'Yer, you'll be lucky all right!' Charles thought it altogether odd but concluded that the man had rather over-indulged in rum tonight. Then something odd happened. Charles turned round to see which way the man was heading but found that he had apparently disappeared into the shadows.

The Tavern   WORKSHEET

Key skills

1. Writing short stories.
2. Creating atmosphere.

Starter activity

1. You wouldn't expect to meet a ghost in a . . .
2. They were scared and all alone in a huge . . .
3. If they really were cut off from the world with these snowdrifts, who was it now coming up to the front door . . .
4. The old grandfather clock was just about to strike midnight when . . .
5. All his life he had never given ghosts a single thought until one evening . . .

Main phase

Read through with the students the extracts on the worksheet. Discuss with them how each story might continue. It is a good idea to jot down notes of the sorts of things that might happen next before writing the next part of the story. Encourage students to experiment, discard, review, rewrite and discuss their ideas with a partner. It doesn't matter if the first attempts are quite short.

Plenary

Hear different versions of the same extract read out. Encourage a discussion about how else the ideas and story line could progress and develop. Ask students to keep a look-out for the parts they like.

Suggestions for homework

Ask the students to choose an extract which they haven't worked on yet. Ask them to write out two (or more) different versions of the same extract.

Suggestions for development of this work

Produce a wall display with the title: 'How will the story continue?' Present the extracts with arrows from it and examples of students' work showing the variety of the ways in which they can be continued.

Extended exercise to develop a KS4 focus based on this work

Ask students to research ghost stories and find an interesting extract. The student can then give a speaking-and-listening presentation to the class to read the extract and point out how the language makes the reader feel scared.

Extended exercise to develop a KS4 focus based on this work

Research and find an interesting extract from a ghost story by the writer M. R. James.

1. Identify the archaic features of the language.
2. Rewrite the passage in a modern style.
3. Write a commentary explaining the changes made.

1. Mr Potter was astonished. He had leant his bicycle up against the tree to deliver his letters, a few moments ago. Now the bicycle was missing. For a postman that is annoying. But that wasn't what worried him. This was now the third time this had happened in two weeks. And always when he delivered post to that particular house. Perhaps the rumours about the ghost were true after all.

2. She came into the room holding the tray of teas and biscuits. She at first held it in a tightened grip. Then she dropped it and there was the awful clatter of broken cups. It was strange, but she didn't scream immediately. It started as a low growl and developed into a scream as if from another world. There in front of her it stood. It was perfectly calm and motionless. Slowly it moved its huge head and looked straight at her. A smile began to appear on its terrifying face.

3. Staying alone in this cottage had not seemed such a big deal. It would only be for one night. But as the wind got up and started to fling the tiles off the roof and as the rain began to lash at the windows and leaks started to appear everywhere, it more and more seemed that the cottage was under attack.

4. The night watchman made his round holding the lead to his mastiff. He knew every inch of that ancient wall. He checked that the stout oak doors were securely locked, lifting his lantern to see. He noticed all the little details in the pale flickering light. What he hadn't noticed, and what his guard dog hadn't yet sensed, was the shape of a monk in a dark hooded cloak advancing on him from behind.

5. The underground train sped through the dark tunnels. Lorna had made the journey many times this late at night and the fact that she was alone in the carriage was not unusual. She had passed Tottenham Court Road and Oxford Circus and now it was just Bond Street and then Marble Arch to go. The train pulled in, rather sooner that she had expected. The platform was deserted. She was reading a poster on the wall when she noticed the name of the station: 'Old Heath'.

   'That's odd,' she thought. 'This should be Bond Street.' The train stood silent. She tried to think of reasons why Bond Street Station would suddenly, without warning, have a name change. She was certain that she had never stopped at any other station on this line in all the years she had travelled it.

   A strange silence hung over the dingy station. She noticed that everything looked rather old-fashioned. But there was something very odd. Everything was new! The tiles, for example looked as if they had just been laid. But everything was so old-fashioned. Then a terrible realization dawned on her . . .

Key skills

1. Creating atmosphere.

Starter

Ask students to write a list of good ingredients for a spooky story.

Main phase

Read through the spooky starters on the worksheet and ask students to chose one and continue it.

Plenary

Arrange for students to read their continuations to the rest of the class.

Suggestions for homework

Students to take home their continuation story and redraft and improve it.

Suggestions for development of this work

Ask students to plan and write a spooky story completely of their own invention.

Extended exercise to develop a KS4 focus based on this work

Students to research and find spooky pictures and then write a story, or a scene from a story, based on the picture. Then students to work in pairs and read each other's work and suggest ways, to each other, of how to enhance the spooky quality of the writing.

Extended exercise to develop a KS5 focus based on this work

Students to research and find a variety of spooky pictures. They then write two scenes from two different genres based on and inspired by the pictures. The two genres are to be: 'romance' and 'ghost'.

They then write a short essay, using the two scenes they have written as a source, in answer to this question: 'How does the vocabulary of a story help to define its genre?'

Start of Story 1

Darren had been to his friend's house playing computer games all evening and it had got later than he'd realized. He set off for home and decided to take a short-cut through a little wooded area. The winter night was icy cold and the moon was full in the sky. Everything looked grey and shadowy. He hadn't ventured far into the wooded area when he felt the full force of the cold penetrating through his clothes. He stopped and looked up at the moon. The lines of the bare branches made strange outlines. As he got further into the woods he remembered something his grandad had once told him, years ago. The unexpected and sudden memory of that gave him a bit of a start. The name of the ancient woods was Blackfriar Woods, he remembered.

'There's talk in the village about the ghost of a friar that wanders around them woods at night. I don't believe all that rubbish,' he had said, but then had added: 'But I'll not go in there at night.'

Start of Story 2

The two boys knew that the old red lighthouse boat moored by the deserted part of the dock was supposed to be haunted. They had made an agreement, as boys do, to nip down to the boat one night and explore it. They had prepared themselves with a torch each. It had really begun as a dare in the comforting sunshine the other day. As they boarded the boat in the dim light and heard the strange strains and creaks deep in the shadows of the vessel they began to wonder if it was a good idea after all. But nothing could have prepared them for what was going to happen that night.

Spooky Starters **WORKSHEET**

Key skills

1. Stage play writing.
2. Creating atmosphere on the stage.

Starter

Ask the students to consider this question: 'If you were staying the night in a spooky country house, what sorts of things would you expect to add to the spooky atmosphere?'

Ask them to write notes for a few minutes.

Main phase

Part 1

Read the worksheet where an example of the beginning of a spooky play is given called 'Bleak Night'.

Explain to the students that a play script is designed to be acted out in front of an audience and a lot of the meaning is conveyed by the way the actors interpret the parts. Experiment with the students acting out the play so far.

Part 2

Ask students to discuss in pairs how the play might develop.

Ask students to write the next part of the play.

Part 3

Ask students to think up their own setting, characters and story line. Ask them to write their own beginning of a play with a spooky atmosphere in the style of the example.

Plenary

Read out some of the continuations of the play 'Bleak Night'.

Suggestions for homework

Ask the students to look up and write out the meanings of ten of the following words. Then get them to produce a poster clearly showing the words and their meanings, together with symbols and small illustrations to make the poster look interesting.

Theatre words: actor; stage manager; scene; lead part; set; prompt; costume; playwright; backdrop; backstage; footlight; green room; audience; character; cue; dress rehearsal; performance; plot; understudy; interpretation.

Suggestions for development of this work

Ask students to describe how the inside of the room might look on a stage.

Draw and colour the stage set.

Design and draw the costumes for the characters.

Extended exercise to develop a KS4 focus based on this work

Arrange for the students to act out the playscript (and their continuation, if possible) in a speaking and listening drama-based session where the focus is to adopt a character.

Extended exercise to develop a KS5 focus based on this work

Ask students to research and select an extract from a classic novel in the ghost genre and rewrite it into a play script format. Write a commentary about the process of changing a scene from a novel into the form of a play.

Characters:

Zina — Visitor caught in a storm
Hannah — Friend of Zina, also caught in a storm
Martin — Butler
Bertram — The master of the house

Set: — The inside of an old house in the remote countryside somewhere near the barren coast of Cornwall. Time: the present.

Zina: (Pushing open the creaky door; there is the sound of the storm outside; the lighting is set at a ghostly yellow; in the hearth a huge fire burns) Hello! Is anybody home? Can we come in, it's terrible out there?

Hannah: (Following timidly) We shouldn't just barge like this into someone's house. I don't like it.

Zina: What else can we do? That weather out there is fearful.

Hannah: Why did that car have to break down like that right in the middle of nowhere?

Zina: And why didn't we remember to charge our phones?

Hannah: Never mind about all that now. (Raising her voice) Hello! Is there anyone at home?

Zina: Look, a blazing fire! That's what we need. (The women go over to the fire and warm their hands. Then they look round the room. The storm is raging outside)

Hannah: Should we just wait here or have a look in other parts of the house for someone?

Zina: I think that we should just wait here. The owner won't mind us sheltering like this. Anyway, the door was open.

Hannah: Look at this. How strange. (Picks up a birthday card from the table)

Zina: What?

Hannah: It's a birthday card.

Zina: I can see that.

Hannah: Yes, but just one. One birthday card. That's odd, isn't it?

Zina: Well, what does it say inside it?

Hannah: (Reads) 'Happy Birthday – Eighty years old eh? That's a miracle considering the life you've led!'

Zina: Look at the card. It's home made isn't it?

Hannah: Yes. Look, there's a picture of a private detective on the front.

Zina: Do you think he was a private detective?

(A dark figure is advancing into the room without the women realizing)

Dark Figure: What business is it of yours?

(The two women scream in shock as they swing round)

Hannah: Sorry, we didn't see you there. We tried to call out. We got stranded in the storm and wondered if we could have a bit of shelter. (The dark figure says nothing but just stares. The sound of the storm resounds outside. Eventually, Hannah continues nervously) Are you the owner?

Dark Figure: No, I am Martin, Bertram's butler. The master will be concerned that you didn't knock.

Zina: We're sorry, the door was open and we called out.

Martin: I shall fetch the master. (He shuffles off slowly out of the door he entered through)

Hannah: He's a bit unfriendly.

Zina: I don't like this one bit. Let's go back to the car and wait in there.

Hannah: We can't do that, it's miles away. We'd get drenched to the bone.

(Enter Bertram)

Bertram: Welcome to my humble abode. I must apologise for Martin my servant. He's a little, er, shall we say disappointed . . . It's his birthday today, you see, and he only received one card. And that was from me.

Section F: Creating Tension

Key skills

1. Short story writing.
2. Creating tension.

Main phase

Part 1

Read through with students the story entitled 'The vase' on the worksheet.

Discuss how it might continue.

Part 2

Ask students to write a continuation of the story, trying to maintain tension.

Plenary

Ask students to read out examples of their continuations.

Suggestions for homework

Ask students to write their own original story which attempts to create tension.

Suggestions for development of this work

Ask students to research and find examples of great literature which creates tension. A good author to explore is John Buchan. Ask students to find a small extract which they like and to read it carefully and try and write down how it creates tension.

Extended exercise to develop a KS4 focus based on this work

Ask around your education establishment to find out if any member of staff enjoys thriller-type writing which creates tension. Ask them if they would select a favourite extract and read it to the class and perhaps explain how they feel and what they think of when they read it.

Extended exercise to develop a KS5 focus based on this work

Ask students to:

1. Select a short extract from John Buchan's *The 39 Steps*.
2. Identify, by close reading, how the writing produces its effects.
3. Locate and find a piece of writing which has a relaxed pace. Compare it to the Buchan example and write a report on how the language works, in the one case to create tension, and in the other, how it creates a sense of calm.
4. Identify particular words and phrases and comment on their effect on the reader.

'It's good of you to call again, Martin. Thank you so much. You're so kind.'

'Not at all, Gladys. What are neighbours for? I've brought you some nice fruit cake. The sort you like. I'll go and pop the kettle on.'

'You are a lovely man, you really are.' Martin pottered in the kitchen with the tea things.

'Martin, I've got something to ask you. A big favour.' Martin came from the kitchen.

'Pardon Gladys, I didn't quite catch that.'

'Oh, it's a bit embarrassing really. My grandchildren are going off on holiday and I'd like to give them some spending money. The only problem is I'm a bit short of cash.'

'No problem, Gladys. Why didn't you say? How much do you need?' And with this Martin pulled out his wallet.

'Oh no, Martin. I don't mean that. Although it's very kind of you. No, what I meant was, could you take a couple of those vases on the sideboard there to Duncan's Antiques in town. He'll give a fair price.' Martin picked up the vases and examined them.

'These, you mean?' he asked, turning them in his hands. 'How much do you want for them?'

'A couple of hundred would be lovely dear.'

'How soon do you need the cash?'

'Oh, in the next couple of days will do.'

'I'll tell you what, Gladys. I know a really good antiques place just round the corner from where I work in the city. They'll give you a really good price for them. I'll take them tomorrow, pop and see him at lunchtime and by this time tomorrow you'll have the cash. How about that?' They smiled at each other. Martin looked back at the vases. They depicted hunting scenes in bright greens and orange. They had an oriental look about them. Martin turned one in his hand. 'Have you had them valued?' he asked casually.

'No, dear. They've been in the family for years but nobody knows much about them.'

'Where did they come from originally?'

'My grandfather brought them back from when he worked on the ships. They were a gift for my mother and she left them to me.' A faint glint appeared in Martin's eye.

'I'd better wrap them up carefully then,' he said. 'Got any bubble wrap?'

The next day Martin set off for London on his usual train with the vases well wrapped up and stowed in a strong leather bag. He went through his usual morning work routine and at lunch time set off for a small antiques shop which he didn't exactly 'know' but had passed its window many a time and had often lingered, looking enviously at the treasures on display.

He entered. A small, thin, bald man rose from the shadows. The man seemed to be summing up the parcels before Martin had taken them from the bag. 'I was wondering if you would be interested in making me an offer for these,' he said. The man nodded with a faint smile but his attention was fixed on the vase as it was unwrapped. Both vases stood on the counter. The man picked up the first one and put it down almost immediately.

'I wouldn't be interested in that one,' he said with a rather subservient nervous voice. 'But this one . . .' he picked it up and produced a magnifying glass from his pocket. He spent a long while examining the vase closely. The shop was silent save for the distant rumbling of traffic outside and the ticking of several clocks. At last he gave a heavy sigh. 'Where did you get this?' he asked.

'A friend,' replied Martin. The man looked at Martin and his expression seemed to say, 'That's what they all say.' 'Well, it's quite rare. I'm prepared to give you ten for it.'

'I'm sorry,' said Martin, deflated. 'It's got to be more than ten pounds. It's very old, you know.'

'I know exactly how old it is,' snapped the man. 'I didn't mean ten pounds of course. I was referring to ten thousand.' Martin was rather stunned and tried to hide it.

'Right, OK, I agree.'

The man produced some paperwork and recorded Martin's details thereon. He asked for some ID. The transaction was quickly resolved and Martin found himself walking out of the shop with one not-so-carefully wrapped vase and a cheque for £10,000 in his pocket. On the way back to work he called at an expensive restaurant which he sometimes went to and ordered himself an expensive meal and a bottle of the best champagne. He couldn't hide the smile on his face and in the afternoon his work colleagues were surprised to see him in such a good mood. He did not, however, explain to anyone why he was so happy.

That evening he called at Gladys' house at around eight.

'Great news, Gladys!' he exclaimed. 'Guess how much?'

'Did you get the 200?' she asked, excited.

'Better than that. Much better. I told you you'd get a fair price, didn't I? Five hundred pounds, the two vases!'

'Oh that's wonderful, Martin. Simply wonderful. I'll be able to give my grandchildren the money now. But you must have something. Martin, I'm going to give you £100!'

The Vase

WORKSHEET

Key skills

1. Writing to explain.

Starter

Ask students to try to think of ten situations where someone would need rescuing. For example, finding yourself stuck in an avalanche.

Main phase

Part 1

Read through with students Part 1.

The danger scenario is given, together with an example of an answer. Discuss with students other ideas they may have to escape such a situation.

Part 2

Read through with students the scenarios in Part 2. Ask them to choose one and write to explain imaginatively how they would escape to safety. Ask them to try to write in the style of the example.

Once they have done one, ask them to choose and do another one.

Plenary

Read out to the class some of their predicaments and their explanations for escape.

Suggestions for homework

Ask students to research and find real-life situations where people have been in a survival situation and escaped to safety (or were rescued) from it. Ask them to make summary notes and then present a brief report to the class explaining clearly what the predicament was and how the problem was solved.

Suggestions for development of this work

Students to research safety procedures for known potentially dangerous situations. They are then to plan, rough-draft and produce best copies of posters which explain clearly the dangers and give advice for sensible safety precautions. For example, riding a bicycle at night.

Extended exercise to develop a KS4 focus based on this work

Ask students to research and produce a page, in their own writing, for a survival guide. They may choose their own situation.

Extended exercise to develop a KS5 focus based on this work

Students to carry out the same activity as the KS4 Focus. They then write a critical commentary detailing presentational features and how effective they are. Ask students to use the critical commentary to experiment and improve and redraft their work.

Part 1

Imagine the following scenario: You are rowing a boat on a river, enjoying yourself. The current is stronger than you think and your boat is swept powerfully downstream. In the panic you lose both oars and then you realize, to your horror, that the edge of the river is approaching fast. The river flows over a waterfall with a sheer drop of over 100 metres. Explain what you do. Use first-person narrative.

Example of an explanation:

I looked in disbelief. My boat was being swept along towards the waterfall. What should I do? If I jump out I will be swept along in the current. If I stay in the boat I'll go over the edge in it. My heart started to pound like crazy. Amazingly, an idea occurred to me in my moment of need. On the bank of the river, to the left was an overhanging branch of a tree. If I could just grab that, I might be saved. But the boat is not heading for the bank. The boat is heading straight down the centre of the river! I then remembered the rudder. The oars were gone but I still had the rudder! I seized it and moved it in such a way as to make the boat veer to the left. As I neared the overhanging branches I made a supreme effort and grabbed at them. I hurled myself to the safety of the bank and caught a glimpse of the empty boat hurtling over the edge. I was saved!

Part 2

Examples of scenarios:

1. You are walking on your own through the countryside. It is a lonely spot and you are getting tired. Suddenly you fall down a disused well and crash down to the bottom. You are slightly injured. How do you get out?
2. You have agreed to be in a play. You haven't told anyone, but for a range of reasons you haven't learned your lines. It is the night of the first performance. You stand there, waiting to go on. You don't know your lines. What do you do?
3. You are lost in a forest at night. It begins to snow and the temperature falls drastically. The wind gets up. Explain what you do.
4. You are on a boat at sea which has been blown away from sight of the coast. Explain what you do.
5. You are the best man at a wedding. The vicar asks you for the ring. You can't find it. What do you do?

Key skills

1. Writing an interior monologue.
2. Creating psychological realism in a character.

Starter activity

Ask students to try to think of five situations where people may typically experience high levels of stress. For example:

1. Just before an actor goes on stage.
2. Waiting in the dentist's waiting room.

Main phase

Part 1

Read through, with the students, the example of Jack waiting at the cinema in the style of an interior monologue.

Explain to the students that an interior monologue is the unfolding of a stream of private thoughts in reaction to a situation. Note some of the characteristics of the language. The thoughts just flow out. There is no formal order. There are a lot of questions. Sometimes the thoughts go in one direction, sometimes in another. The growing stressful situation intensifies the thought process. There is reaction to what is happening around the person at that time.

Part 2

Read through the suggested situations and ask students to choose one and write an interior monologue in the style of the example.

Plenary

Ask students to read out their interior monologues to the class.

Suggestions for homework

Ask students to produce a chart of ten stressful situations and against each one a brief note of how the person may have felt at the time. These will be like mini interior monologues.

Suggestions for development of this work

Investigate autobiographies of famous and successful people. Select a time in their life from the autobiography when they were stressed. Ask students to imagine that they were the person and write a short interior monologue, in the style of the worked example.

Extended exercise to develop a KS4 focus based on this work

Ask students to watch a drama on TV and to imagine that they were one of the main characters, if possible, in a stressful situation. Then ask them to write a brief interior monologue of that character in the style we have been exploring.

Extended exercise to develop a KS5 focus based on this work

Ask students to choose a passage in a great piece of literature and imagine that they were one of the main characters. Ask them to write an interior monologue based on that character's situation. For example, in the opening of *Far from the Madding Crowd* by Thomas Hardy, Farmer Oak is described. Students to write an interior monologue, as if they were Farmer Oak, describing his daily life.

Being under stress monologue

Scenario: Jack has arranged to meet his new girlfriend outside the cinema at ten to eight one Friday evening. He is waiting.

Jack's internal monologue:

7.45 I'm really excited about this. She agreed so quickly. Fantastic. She's so pretty.

Now let me think. Outside the cinema at ten to eight. She will know that I mean the front of the cinema, won't she? Of course she will. Shall I pay for the tickets? Yes, I think that would be the right thing to do. What about sweets? I know, she can choose her favourites and I'll buy them.

7.50 Any moment now . . . I think this watch is correct. What does that clock inside the cinema say? Oh dear, it's nearer to five to eight on the cinema clock. Where is she then? Is that her? No, it's someone who looks like her. I wonder how she'll be getting here? Maybe she's held up. I'm sure there will be a simple explanation. I wonder what she'll be wearing. Do I look smart enough?

8.00 What do I do now? It's now eight o'clock! I feel such a fool. Everyone else is going in. They're looking at me as if to say: 'Poor boy, she's stood him up.'

8.05 There is only one cinema in town, isn't there? Yes, there is only one. So, where on earth is she? Should I just go in on my own? Should I just go home? What will I say to her when I next see her? No, don't panic, she'll turn up. It's only a few minutes anyway. She's just been held up, that's all. There'll be a good explanation. (Pause) But why didn't she phone me? Of course, she hasn't got my number has she? Oh, Holly, please, please turn up.

8.10 Well, this is getting serious now. It looks like maybe she has forgotten, after all. Now let me think about this. She likes Darren, doesn't she? She's always smiling at him and being nice, I know that. Maybe she's gone out with him instead. No, these are silly thoughts! She looked so keen when I asked her, she really did. Still, why have I got this horrible feeling of disappointment growing in my stomach? Maybe I'm just not up to her standards. Maybe she was just humouring me? I must stop pacing about like this. Oh dear, look at the time.

8.15 Well, that's it. She's not coming now, is she? I'm going home. I don't think it would have worked out with us anyway. It just didn't feel right somehow. I'm just a bit of a fool, that's all!

Note: just then a taxi pulls up in a hurry and Holly jumps out and charges up to Jack. She says: 'I'm so sorry Jack, my dad couldn't start his car so I had to get a taxi. Sorry you were kept waiting so long. We can still catch the film can't we? It's just the trailers we've missed.'

Being Under Stress Monologue **WORKSHEET**

Key skills
1. Short story writing.
2. Creating tension.

Starter
Ask students to think of stories which build up tension. Maybe they can think of films or TV programmes they have seen. List three stories.

Have they any suggestions on how tension is built up? Ask them to make a few notes. Can they think of any suitable sentences or phrases which would be useful in writing a story which included mounting tension?

Main phase
Part 1
Read through with the class the short story called 'Someone is following me' on the worksheet.
Part 2
Ask students to continue the story in their own words. They may wish to jot down notes about the sorts of things that might happen next.
Part 3
Ask students to write their own story which gradually builds up tension.

Plenary
Read their continuations and own stories to the class.

Suggestions for homework
Ask students to research and find a story which builds up tension. They then copy out an extract and comment on how it builds up tension. Share examples together as a class.

Suggestions for development of this work
Arrange for the class to produce a series of wall posters which include examples of writing which build up tension. Also have the students produce posters for tips and advice for building up tension.

Extended exercise to develop a KS4 focus based on this work
Ask students to rewrite the story 'Someone is Following Me' from the point of view of the woman in the red scarf.

Extended exercise to develop a KS5 focus based on this work
Ask students to read a mystery by the author Francis Durbridge and to give a presentation to the rest of the group which outlines the story line, highlighting a part of the writing which creates tension. They then explain, in detail, by close examination of the language, how the tension is created.

Someone is following me

Friends Harry and Charlie went to London for the day to see the sights. They got off the train and walked by the side of the River Thames, chatting and laughing as friends do. They found a cafe and ordered coffees and cakes.

'Isn't it amazing?' said Charlie, gazing out of the window at the floods of people rushing by. 'All these people. You glance at them and then never see them again. Strange to think that.'

'You might see them again,' said Harry, sipping his cappuccino.

'You might do, but to be honest it's unlikely, isn't it?' Charlie watched the people marching past. One woman stood out, but only for a fraction of a second. She was middle aged and had a red scarf wrapped round her head. Her face was half hidden. Charlie didn't really know why the woman stood out.

'Each one has their own life, their own friends, their own world,' said Charlie, half dreamily.

The boys finished their snacks and set off down Fleet Street full of energy and eager curiosity. They discussed the places they would like to visit that day.

The first place was the Aquarium. They were fascinated to be up so close against mighty sharks which swept past them. Charlie noticed a face reflected in the glass, and swung round. The woman with the red scarf was standing there, watching the sharks. 'Now that is strange,' he thought. After what we had said in the cafe about never seeing the same people again.

The boys moved on and went on the London Eye, visited Churchill's bunker and a museum. They decided to have lunch in a fast-food restaurant. Charlie had forgotten to tell Harry about the strange coincidence until he suddenly stopped eating his chips, and froze.

'What is it?' asked Harry.

'That woman again.'

'What woman?'

'That woman with the red headscarf. She just passed the window and looked in at us.'

'What woman?' asked Harry, genuinely confused.

'I didn't tell you at the time, but a woman passed the cafe we were in earlier, wearing a red scarf. I saw her again in the Aquarium and then I just saw her look through this window. Harry, I think we're being followed.'

'Don't be silly,' said Harry. 'There must be millions of women in London wearing red scarves.'

'No, it was definitely the same woman,' said Charlie. 'I think we're being followed!'

That afternoon the two of them strolled up to Buckingham Palace and went down Oxford Street. They decided to take a river trip as the sun had come out and it was pleasant outdoors and they had felt so crushed up in the shops.

It was while they were on the river trip, gliding past the Houses of Parliament, that Charlie grabbed Harry's hand and nodded in the direction of the approaching bridge. A woman, wearing a red head scarf, was on the bridge, holding a camera and pointing it directly at them. She stood perfectly still with the camera obscuring her face.

'Now do you believe me?' asked Charlie, quite disturbed by now.

'Well, it does seem a bit odd, I must admit. Perhaps she is following us. Maybe she's one of those strange people who just follow random people around. I don't know.'

The boys decided to get off the tour cruiser as soon as they could and confront the woman. But, by the time that had got to the bridge, she was nowhere to be seen.

They worked out that they only had time for one more place to visit before they would have to get the train home. It was a choice between Madame Tassaud's and the London Dungeon. They decided on the London Dungeon. By the time they got there, dark clouds had began to form in the sky and the bright and cheerful day had now changed to a depressing grey light. They paid their entrance fees and entered the dungeon . . .

Key skills

1. Letter writing.
2. Engaging reader's interest with the unexpected element.

Starter

Explain to students that sometimes things don't go to plan and the unexpected happens. Students to discuss with each other for a few minutes something in their own lives that happened unexpectedly.

Main phase

Part 1

Read through with the students the letter which explains an unexpected event.

Part 2

Read through the suggestions of ideas for an unexpected event. Ask students to either choose one from the list or think of one themselves and then write a letter describing and explaining what happened in an interesting way.

Plenary

Ask students to read out some of their letters to the class. Ask students to look out for particularly interesting parts.

Suggestions for homework

Ask students to chat to their parents and guardians and ask them if they can recall an unexpected event in their lives. Students to take notes and then a session can be arranged where the students briefly present the highlights of their family's unexpected experiences to the rest of the class.

Suggestions for development of this work

Arrange for students to read some biographies of famous people and look out for events which were unexpected. Students to produce a letter, to a friend, as if they were the famous person, describing the event, using the information from the biography.

Extended exercise to develop a KS4 focus based on this work

Students to write a letter from the viewpoint of a disgruntled customer, in a formal style, to the management of the Ogilvey Theatre complaining about the incident. They then compare that letter with the letter in the worksheet, which is written in an informal style, to a friend about the unexpected event. They are then to write a detailed answer to this question: 'What are the similarities and differences between formal and informal writing?'

Extended exercise to develop a KS5 focus based on this work

Students to choose one of the situations, not worked on yet, from Part 2 of the worksheet. They are then to write a letter to a friend, explaining fully the event, using direct quotes of what people had said and then rewrite the letter using only reported speech. Students are then to read each other's pairs of letters in direct and reported speech and then write an essay answering this question: 'How does the reader's experience change when reported speech is used instead of direct speech?'

Part 1

The Greg Nash sold out concert

Jo had arranged to see, at a local theatre, a famous singer called Greg Nash. He had looked forward to it for months. Something unexpected happened. He wrote the following letter to his friend about the event:

Dear Alex,

You'll never guess in a million years what happened! You know I had been looking forward to seeing Greg Nash at the Ogilvey Theatre on Friday evening, well he didn't turn up, but something amazing happened.

An old bloke came out on the stage holding a microphone, and the atmosphere was so exciting. The noise of cheering was something else! We were all thinking, Greg Nash is actually in this very building! After all these years I'm going to get the chance to see him live. I had seen him on TV loads of times and you know I've got his entire CD collection. Well, you can imagine how I felt when the old bloke said that Greg had been unavoidably detained due to personal reasons, or something, and instead they had a local girl to sing a few songs from a nearby college.

Well, all I can say is that there was a riot. People demanded their money back. People were screaming and losing their tempers. It was frightening, Alex, I'm telling you. I felt sorry for the girl. She must have been standing in the wings feeling terrible. Loads of people did leave the auditorium and demanded their money back from the box office staff. But I stayed. There were about 30 of us who stayed.

The man came again, onto the stage, and I tell you, Alex, I felt sorry for him. He was all shaky and flustered. He said, in a trembling voice, that in the circumstances there would be no show tonight and he apologized most sincerely on behalf of all the management.

I stood up and said that it wasn't his fault and there were still about 30 of us left so we'd love to hear her sing. The man shuffled off and we could hear a hurried conversation in the wings. A man with a clipboard and earphones popped his head round the curtain and then the old bloke came back. He took a deep breath, gave a smile and said: 'Ladies and gentleman, it gives me great pleasure to introduce to you a new name in the world of pop music. She will singing her own songs tonight. Ladies and gentleman, put your hands together and let's hear it for . . . Chelsie Sparks!'

Although there were only a few of us, we cheered as much as we could and the most beautiful woman I have ever seen walked onto that stage wearing an amazing pink dress. For over an hour she charmed us all with a voice from heaven. I didn't so much walk out of the theatre that night as float out in a state of enchantment. Alex, you know me, I'm not easily impressed, but this lady was incredible. Who cares about Greg Nash, I'd rather see her any time!

But that's not all of it. The best bit is yet to come. As I was walking through the car park outside, someone held my arm and I heard these words: 'Thank you for what you did tonight. Maybe this is my lucky break?' There she was. Alex, can you believe what I'm saying here? She came out to find me because of what I'd stood up and said. Well, we got chatting, and guess what? I'm seeing her next week. We're going for a meal. Can you believe that?

Please write back and tell me what you think. I love unexpected things, don't you?

Your friend,

Jo

Part 2

Suggestions of ideas for an unexpected event:

1. You are the only passenger travelling on a bus one evening, on your way to visit a friend. You walk to the back of the bus and sit down. There, next to you, is an old-looking, tatty leather bag. You casually glance inside and find to your utter surprise that it is stuffed with thousands of pounds of cash. What happens next?

2. You are invited to a friend's wedding. You take a taxi to the church. When you get there you realize to your horror that you had forgotten that the clocks had gone forward one hour. The wedding was over and all the people had gone. What happens next?

3. You are enjoying a river cruise down the Thames in London. The boat is very crowded with tourists. Suddenly you stare at one of the tourists. His face is definitely the one that you saw an hour ago on a 'Police Wanted' poster. What happens next?

4. You are in hospital recovering from an operation. Late one night you make your way to the toilets, but on the way you chance to overhear a night porter making a secret phone call. This is what you hear: 'Yes boss, everything's ready. Yes boss, my disguise as a porter worked a treat; fooled everyone! The medicine store is full and I've got hold of the keys. There must be a fortune's worth in there! If you bring the van round at the time we said I'll be ready for you. It should only take a few minutes to load it . . .' What happens next?

Unexpected Event **WORKSHEET**

71

5. One morning you are excited to receive a card that says the following: 'Dear nephew, happy birthday! Come over to my house where I've got a special present for you. With love , Uncle Charles.' You can't wait to get over there. Your uncle is a scientist and inventor and you imagine all sorts of wonderful presents. What could it be? When you get there you are surprised and disappointed to find that the present is two small bottles, one containing blue liquid, the other containing red. But your uncle explains that one drop of the blue on any object will increase its size by tenfold; one drop of the red will do the opposite – any object will shrink by tenfold. Your uncle says: 'Happy birthday! – Go and have fun with them!' What happens next?

6. You are at the funfair and take a ride in a ghost train. Halfway round, the carriage stops suddenly and all the power goes out. Everything is plunged into pitch darkness . A door opens and a cloaked figure emerges from a gloomy green interior and beckons you in. You enter another world, not of the ghost train any more, but of a world of real ghosts. What happens next?

7. You enter a nationwide competition to design a birthday card for the Queen. You spend a lot of time designing and producing it and then you submit your entry. Incredibly, you find out two months later that your entry wins! You are invited to Buckingham Palace to meet the Queen and present the card to her. What happens next?

8. You are visiting the Ancient Egyptian Pyramids and the tour guide takes your party deep into the massive vaults. The air is icy cold. Without warning a huge block of stone falls into the doorway, sealing the vault! The tourists' reaction is to laugh, thinking that it is a stunt. But the tour guide looks shocked. He says: 'Oh God! That has never happened before! We're all prisoners!' What happens next?

9. You have waited a long time to see your favourite pop star in concert. At last the day arrives! As you enter the stadium each member of the audience is handed a special raffle ticket. The idea is that at the end of the concert a number will be called and the lucky winner will get the chance to go backstage and meet the star. The time comes for the calling of the number. It is yours! What happens next?

10. You attend a medieval reconstruction at a country castle one summer's day. Lots of performers have dressed up in medieval costume and you have a great time. When the time comes to go home you are surprised that instead of a bus, a horse and carriage arrives to pick you up. Then it slowly dawns on you that something unbelievable has happened. You have been transported back to the year 1209. What happens next?

Section G: The World of Feelings

Key skills
1. Writing to describe.
2. Writing with a theme as central to the creative process.

Starter
Ask students to make a list of the weather conditions which would prevent you, or discourage you, from venturing outside.

Main phase
Part 1
Read through the worked example on the worksheet entitled 'Cosy inside'.
Part 2
Read through the situations and ask them to choose one to write about.
Part 3
Guide them through the suggested step-by-step process as shown.

Plenary
Ask students to read out extracts from the best parts of their work.

Suggestions for homework
Ask students to take one of the example situations and draw an illustration with a dividing line between the two contrasting parts. Label the illustration with as many contrasting words as possible.

Suggestions for development of this work
Ask students to interview a family member about any really bad weather they may have been caught up in, once. Suggest that the student takes some key point notes. Then ask the student to write up a description of the bad weather and the contrast with the shelter taken (in the style of this work). The student can then show the finished result to the family member who may possibly write a comment.

Extended exercise to develop a KS4 focus based on this work
Ask students to research and find examples from great literature of outstanding descriptive writing. Ask students to copy out a small extract and then select particularly good examples of descriptive sentences. Comment on why they are good sentences.

Extended exercise to develop a KS4 focus based on this work
Ask students to write an extended description of a landscape in all four seasons, with special regard to the weather conditions. Then, working with a partner, experiment with the process of redrafting, editing and improving. Compare the first draft to the finished copy and comment on why particular language changes were made and what effect they had on the reader.

Part 1

Example: 'Cosy inside'

I was woken up by the train stopping its movement. I was lulled by the rhythm of the movement and now it had stopped. Had we arrived already? Surely not. I looked at my watch. It was half-past three in the morning. I pulled back the curtain in my sleeping compartment from the window and looked at my own reflection in the black, steamed-up glass. I got out of bed, slipped on my dressing gown and ventured out to see what was going on. People were stirring from their beds, and as I passed one compartment in the corridor I heard a weather report on the radio and I caught the words 'snow' and 'blizzard'. A member of rail staff was coming my way along the corridor with a silver tray with tea things on it.

'I'm afraid we're snowed in,' he said as he passed. I noticed his face was red and he seemed harassed. I got to one of the outside doors. I opened it and looked out. The snow was raging, and from the light of the train I could see a thick layer of snow stretching back into the darkness. The snow falling in the light of the doorway reminded me of one of those ornaments which you shake and then watch all the snow swirl round. I shivered as invisible frozen hands grabbed at me from the frozen night. I shut the door and decided that the best thing would be to go back to my warm bunk-bed. I wonder if I could order a hot cup of hot chocolate?

Part 2

Choose one of the following situations and write about it in detail:

1. You are in an overnight long-distance sleeper train thundering along in the night, and outside a snow storm is raging. So much snow has piled up on the track that the train has to come to a stop in the middle of a wilderness in Scotland.
2. You are snuggled up in your sleeping-bag in a tent and outside on the moor the thick fog is swirling.
3. You are inside a huge cool banqueting hall in an ancient castle. Outside, the Spanish summer is unbearably hot.
4. You are driving a car in the countryside and a fantastic thunder and lightning storm is raging around you.
5. You are on a tourist sight-seeing boat being served cola and ice while outside in the tropical river you see huge water serpents swirling and crocodiles looking menacingly up at you from the green waters.
6. You are in a nice cosy warm bed and outside the rain is lashing and the wind is howling.

Part 3

A step-by-step process

Step 1

Jot down notes and key words, questions, suggestions and thoughts about inside and outside.

Set them out in a chart.

Here are some possible ideas:

Inside the sleeper train	Outside in the snow storm
1. How was I woken?	1. When I looked out, what did the light from the train show?
2. What did I see out of the window?	2. What could the snow storm be compared to?
3. What time was it?	3. What device could I express the feeling of cold with?
4. Where did I move to and what did I see? Who did I meet?	
5. What were others doing?	
6. Was there a radio? Where? What did I hear?	

Step 2

Try to write out in one sentence the main contrast you are trying to show.
Example: I am trying to show the contrast between the warm, comforting, noisy, people-filled inside compared to the silent, barren wasteland outside with its sense of danger and desolation.

Step 3

Write out a rough draft using ideas from the chart. (Develop each key word or phrase into a sentence.)

Inside and Outside **WORKSHEET**

Key skills

1. Writing to advise.

Starter activity

Explain to students that life is full of problems of one sort or another. Ask them to list ten problems that students of their age commonly experience.

Main phase

Part 1

1. Mention that sometimes people write to teenage magazines to seek advice and help.
2. Ask students to read the Agony Aunt example letters on the worksheet.
3. Ask students to discuss the advice they might offer and suggest that they jot down notes.
4. Students to then write a reply. Once that is done, ask students to choose another letter and write another reply and so on.

Part 2

Once a few letters have been written, ask students to work in pairs where one student writes a letter asking for advice about a problem they may have (or imagined) and the partner reads this and then writes a suitable reply in an appropriate style.

You may wish to get the students to write on separate sheets of paper with reference numbers and distribute them around the class so that nobody knows who they are writing to. You then maintain your own list of reference numbers with the students' names recorded against them so that you can easily cross reference. (A seating plan is essential to manage this one.)

Plenary

Students to hear a few good examples of replies read out to the class.

Suggestions for homework

Ask students to research Agony Aunt letters and replies from magazines and analyse them.

Suggestions for development of this work

Select an Agony Aunt/Uncle letter from the examples and write a character study of the imagined person who wrote it.

Extended exercise to develop a KS4 focus based on this work

Imagine that your school has developed a confidential 'unit' where specially trained staff are available to give advice confidentially to any student who requires it. Explain to the students that they have been given the task of designing and producing a leaflet to be distributed in the school to let everybody know about the service. Ask them to design such a leaflet and then comment on the presentational devices used.

Extended exercise to develop a KS5 focus based on this work

Ask students to write a full letter to an Agony Aunt in a magazine as if written by a teenager. Then ask them to write a letter, as if from an experienced teacher who is experiencing her own problems, to the Samaritans. Now compare the letters and write a report on the contrasting features of the style of language used.

1. Dear Agony Aunt/Uncle,

   I hate school. It is as simple as that. I find the work boring and I'm often just gazing out of the windows. My mum has warned me that if I carry on like this I'll end up with no qualifications and get a dead-end job. I'm worried about this situation. I'm wondering if there are any tips you could suggest which might help me improve the situation.

   Yours sincerely,

   David Gower, London

2. Dear Agony Aunt/Uncle,

   Recently my best friend has decided to ignore me. If I say anything about it, she just laughs and says 'Don't be so silly.' It's really starting to get me down. What should I do?

   Yours sincerely,

   Katy Barker, Bristol

3. Dear Agony Aunt/Uncle,

   My mum finds fault with every little thing I do. For example, the other day I poured out the cornflakes and a few missed the plate and landed on the table. She went mad, yelling things like: 'I have to clear up after you all the time!' I'm beginning to get to the stage where I'm nervous to do anything. What should I do?

   Yours sincerely,

   Stephanie Rogers, Norwich

4. Dear Agony Aunt/Uncle,

   My friends are mainly my older brother's friends who are three years older than me. They treat me as one of them. Recently they've started getting into minor troubles with the police and they are encouraging me to join in with them. I feel that I don't want to break the law, but I also want to keep them as friends. What do you think I should do?

   Yours sincerely,

   Jimmy Dawrant, Canterbury

5. Dear Agony Aunt/Uncle,

   I'm not good at science and I worked out a way to cheat in a science exam. I wrote a load of answers on slips of paper which I balanced on my leg and managed to glance at them without the teachers suspecting anything. I ended up getting top marks! The problem is that big Chad the school bully saw me yesterday and said: 'I saw you cheating, you little squirt! Twenty pounds by Friday or the teacher finds out!' My parents were so pleased that I got top marks and now I'm worried and don't know what to do. Please help!

   Yours sincerely,

   Aaron Wilkinson, Birmingham

6. Dear Agony Aunt/Uncle,

   I've noticed lately that I worry about everything. My dad has been in hospital and I'm worried that he won't get better. My school work is not that good and I think the teachers think I'm a failure (I can tell by the way they look at me). My bike-ride to school has become a nightmare because I think someone is going to knock me down; the drivers drive like idiots round my way. The worse thing at the moment is my boyfriend. I feel sure he's seeing another girl, although he denies it. Why did he have a smell of perfume on his clothes the other day? I've realized that lately I lie awake at night with my thoughts chasing round and round. What should I do?

   Yours sincerely,

   Pauline Frosty, Cambridge

   PS: Please reply quickly as I'm worried my letter might get lost in the post!

Key skills

1. Writing a short story in the romance genre.

Starter

Write out a list of films and TV programmes which involve a love story as a central theme.

Main phase

Part 1

Read through the worked example called 'Ben and Jessica' on the worksheet. Discuss with students what might happen next. Ask students to continue the story in writing. It doesn't matter if they don't write a complete story. Just carry on as far as they can.

Part 2

Read through the 'Love story situation' and ask students to write the next part.

Part 3

Ask students to have a go at writing their own love story from scratch.

Plenary

Ask students to write a list of elements of a good love story.

Suggestions for homework

Request students to research and find an extract from a published love story. It can be any kind of love story: a traditional classic or a modern love story. The opening of a story can work very well for this exercise. Ask them to look carefully at the language and write some comments on how it works well as a love story. How does it engage the reader's interest?

Suggestions for development of this work

Joint class research project. Ask each member of the class to find a small extract from the middle of a love story. Ask them to prepare a short talk which includes the following:

1. A brief summary of the story so far.
2. A reading of the brief extract to the class.
3. A highlighting of a particular phrase or sentence and an explanation of why it is well written.

Extended exercise to develop a KS4 focus based on this work

Ask students to imagine that they are Ben, Jessica, or the shop assistant. Write an informal diary note expressing how they feel about the events of that day.

Extended exercise to develop a KS5 focus based on this work

Ask students to take a piece of writing where the example of the Ben and Jessica story has been developed and extended by them. Imagine Ben is interviewed for a magazine feature entitled: 'Is this true love?'

Write out the interview. From the written interview consider the following and write notes on each one:

1. What is the purpose of the interview?
2. How does the interviewer influence the outcomes with the way the questions are styled?
3. Describe the intended audience and comment on how the style of the interview could cater for that audience.

Suggest ways in which the interview could be presented on the page and comment on the thinking behind the suggestions.

Part 1

Ben and Jessica

Ben has been seeing Jessica for several years. They did get on quite well, although lately they have been arguing more and drifting apart a little. Ben is in the habit of buying regular presents for Jessica, like roses and chocolates. For a while after the present is given the relationship improves a little, but as time has gone by she has been getting less and less impressed by the presents so that he has had to spend more and more of his overtime money to buy more expensive presents. One day, during his lunch hour, he is in a high quality sweet shop when the following happens . . .

'Thank you, Sir. Did you know that this is the most expensive luxury box of chocolates we stock? Who's the lucky person?' The assistant smiled warmly at Ben.

'Well, a friend of mine.' Ben stood slightly awkwardly.

'She'll be thrilled!'

'No she won't!' Ben didn't quite know why he had suddenly said that. It was one of those moments when an impulsive thought bursts its way out. The woman looked quite taken aback. Ben thought about the times when his offerings had been discarded without much acknowledgement – and particularly lately. There were only the two of them standing in the shop at that moment. Ben looked at the brightly coloured wrappings behind the woman and seemed to enter into a dreamlike state. Strangely, he felt a little better actually saying what had been lurking deep down for some time.

'Well, I would be thrilled,' she said.

'Then they're yours!'

'Don't be silly.' She smiled again and began the mechanical process of wrapping. 'Gift wrapped?'

'I'm serious,' said Ben. 'You'll appreciate them. She won't. Please, I'm serious. I would be very happy if you would accept these as a gift from me.' Ben had been visiting this shop for a while now and each time he had looked into the assistant's eyes she had appeared that much more pretty. There was a strange combination, right at that moment, of how fresh and lovely she looked combined together with her appreciative attitude and smile that seemed to melt Ben into an emotional fool. 'Please have them,' he said, and offered her the money.

The woman realized in a sudden flash that this man was serious. She looked at the chocolates and then at Ben. 'That is the most wonderful thing that has happened to me,' she said in a burst of joy. She ran round the counter to him, gave him a huge hug and said quietly: 'Thank you.'

Part 2

Love story situation

Two people, Claire and Tony, get married when they are both 18. Things don't go well and for one reason or another they split up after just six months. Both of them then go on to have strangely similar, but totally separate lives. They both get married, have children, get divorced, get married again and then split up again. One day, 30 years after they last saw each other, Tony is in a bustling cafe and sits down at a table on his own. Somebody sits down next to him.

'Hello, Tony, it is you isn't it?' He looks up and with something of a shock recognizes the woman in front of him as being none other than Claire.

True Love

WORKSHEET

Key skills

1. Writing to describe events and feelings in response.

Starter

Ask students to make notes on the sort of perfect day they would like to have in an ideal world.

Main phase

Part 1

Read through the example on the worksheet of someone's perfect day.

Part 2

Ask students to have a go at writing out their own perfect day in the style of the example.

If they are stuck for ideas, ask them to look at and consider ideas from the suggestion list.

Remind them to describe the events in detail.

Plenary

Ask students to read out to the class their perfect day.

Suggestions for homework

Ask students to ask a member of their family if they could interview them and jot down notes for that person's idea of a perfect day. Try to get as many details as possible. Then ask the student to write up the notes into a full account of the perfect day and ask the family member to read it and comment on how well it has been done. It could be written in third person, for example: 'My father's perfect day would be . . .'

Suggestions for development of this work

Arrange for your students to interview teachers in the school and ask them what that teacher's idea of a perfect day might be. Ask the students to jot down notes for that teacher's idea of a perfect day. Try to get as many details as possible. Then ask the student to write up the notes into a full account of the perfect day and ask the teacher to read it and comment on how well it has been done.

Once the perfect days are written up, compile a book which includes them. Have a class competition to see who can design the best cover for the book.

Extended exercise to develop a KS4 focus based on this work

Arrange for the class to become a magazine production team. Each student is allocated a task. The title will be called 'Perfect Days'. Compile together the examples of perfect days from students, teachers and family members. Edit the articles. Add in pictures and headings. Additional information can be added to include: word searches, cartoons, letters to editor, advice on travelling, adverts for items needed for 'perfect days', etc.

Extended exercise to develop a KS5 focus based on this work

The activity here is the same as for KS4 suggestion above but perhaps with greater variety of content, more developed details and a commentary on the magazine when finished.

Part 1

A teacher was asked what his perfect day would be in an ideal world.

This is what he said:

My perfect day would be to wake up in a nice country hotel in Scotland. I would be staying with my wife. I would take a hot shower and then get dressed and go down for a full breakfast. The breakfast would consist of a sausage, a rasher of bacon (not too salty), a fried egg and toast and marmalade washed down by hot, strong tea. I would then venture into the fresh bracing air of a warm Scottish summer's morning. The birds would be singing sweet songs and the sun would be casting a brilliant light across the purple moors. I would feel fully alive and eager to enjoy the day.

My wife and I would then get into our vintage car and drive through the beautiful dramatic countryside to the castle which nestles on the edge of Loch Ness. I would enjoy exploring the remains of this ancient castle. Then I would take some photographs of the area. It would then be nice to sit back and relax and enjoy the feeling of peace. This would be followed by a gentle stroll along the banks of the loch.

For lunch we would visit a picturesque little village set back from the banks of the loch and buy some hot crusty bread from the bakery. We would stock up on juicy sweet ham and home-made cake and then find a picnic spot to enjoy the food. During the picnic it would be great to observe the wildlife. For example, a couple of otters may well be playing around by the side of a stream. We would feel privileged to be able to observe them at such close quarters.

The evening of my perfect day would be to dress up in smart new clothes and visit a local pub where we could chat with some friends and tell each other stories and later in the evening, perhaps indulge in a bit of a sing-song.

Part 2

Suggestions for the perfect day

1. Seeing a favourite football team play and meeting the players afterwards.
2. Seeing a favourite singer and meeting up with the singer after the concert and receiving VIP treatment.
3. Visiting an interesting place for the day.
4. Meeting an old friend or family member who you haven't seen for a while.
5. Getting involved with a favourite sport and being coached by a favourite sportsman.
6. Getting involved with an adventure activity with some friends.

My Perfect Day **WORKSHEET**

Key skills

1. Writing to describe with a focus on sound.
2. Revealing character through their response to sound.

Starter

Ask students to list five sounds they like and five which they dislike. See if they can make a comment against each one explaining why they like or dislike it. Perhaps it evokes a memory?

Main phase

Part 1

Read through, with the students reading the parts, the mini play called 'Sound scapes' in the worksheet.

Part 2

Ask students to think of a small group of people and a setting for them and write out a mini play where the characters talk about their favourite sounds and explain why they like them. Ask them to model it on the style of the example mini play.

Plenary

Arrange for students to read, in role, parts of their plays. Encourage a discussion with the focus on how sounds can open up new areas of imaginative description and also how they can reveal character in a powerful way.

Suggestions for homework

Students to write out a chart with three columns and eleven rows. At the top of the columns they write three headings: Sound; Description; What I think of when I hear the sound. Ask students to complete the chart for homework. Encourage them to find a wide variety of sounds.

For example:

Sound	Description	What I think of when I hear the sound
Waves rolling in.	There is a distant roar, then a surge of watery energy, then a crash and a scraping of shingle . . . and so on . . .	Holidays on the beach with nanny . . . and so on . . .

Suggestions for development of this work

Students to find small extracts from great works of literature. Research them a little. Then read through the extract carefully, copy it onto a piece of paper and suggest the sounds which might be going on in the background of that particular scene. Students to write out their ideas.

Extended exercise to develop a KS4 focus based on this work

Students to write a character description with the emphasis on sound.

Extended exercise to develop a KS5 focus based on this work

Students to construct an oral narrative. Ask them to arrange permissions for family members to be taped having a short conversation about sounds. If the conversation sags, the student could be ready with a few prompt questions, like 'What is the first sound you remember?' Encourage them to try to tell a real-life short story based on a sound. Then write out the transcript of the conversation word for word. Produce a chart in response to the transcript, setting out comments in response to sociolinguist William Labov's ideas about oral narratives:

1. Summarize the key point of the story.
2. Was the story flat, or did it develop?
3. Which part of the story is interesting?
4. How does it end? Does it have a clear ending?

Part 1
Sound scapes

Description of stage. Bare and stark with no scenery. A plain backdrop where different coloured lighting can be thrown. A sound system. A single sign at the side of the stage reads 'Park'.

The scene is a park on a summer's day.

Becky is standing, looking around, when Jess rushes in.

Jess: I'm sorry I'm late.

Becky: You're not normally late. What held you up?

Jess: It's silly really. My cat Billy was on my bed purring and I love the sound of purring.

Becky: You were late because your cat was purring?

Jess: I know it sounds silly, but I've had a lot on my mind lately and the cat's purring has helped me.

Becky: How?

Jess: Well, there's something comforting about a cat purring. It's the rhythm of it. It reminds me of when I was a child, safe in bed with the cat purring. The cat was called 'Jinks' in those days. Jinks was a wild cat that my mum saved from being drowned. It had a lovely purr. The purr was a sort of strange language which seemed to say: 'I was going to be drowned but now I am safe. My purr shows I'm happy again.' (Pause for thought) Have you got a favourite sound?

Becky: Yes, as a matter of fact I have. I love music.

Jess: But is there a particular type of music you like? (The sound of birdsong in the background becomes louder. The two girls stand and listen) Listen to that. I love the sound of birds. Their music is the most natural and wonderful in the world. The world would be a horrible place without birdsong. We take it for granted and mostly we don't even notice it.

(Enter Mike and Todd)

Mike: There you are. We've been looking everywhere for you.

Todd: It's a beautiful day now, isn't it? Where shall we sit and have this picnic?

Jess: We've been talking about our favourite sounds and why we like them. What are your favourite sounds?

Mike: I like the sound of motorbikes.

Becky: Let's sit down and have our picnic here. This is a nice spot. Now Mike, we're playing a sort of game. Explain, in detail if you can, why you like the sound of a motorbike.

Mike: Well, my dad was a mechanic and he used to fix motorbikes as a sideline in our garage at home. When I heard the roar of a motorbike engine I knew he was happy, tinkering about. He loved tinkering about on motorbikes.

Jess: But I think motorbikes sound awful. (The sound of a motorbike rises and falls in the background)

Mike: (Lost in thought) He could tell from the sound how the engine was. He used to say to me: 'You hear that tiny whurr inside that roar? That means the so and so is worn . . .' He was very clever.

Jess: How about you Todd?

Todd: The wind in the trees, I suppose. (Pause) We used to live at the edge of a camping site and the border of the site was thick with trees. When the wind blew you could hear the leaves rustling. They sounded like chips frying in a pan.

Becky: (Closes her eyes) That's good. I can imagine that. (Sounds of rustling trees rise in the background)

Jess: Anyone want a ham sandwich?

Favourite Sounds **WORKSHEET**

83

Key skills

1. Writing descriptively about views of landscape.

Starter

Write down a list of five places where there would be a good view.

Discuss with students this question: When a house is being sold or a holiday destination advertised, you sometimes see the expression: 'Breathtaking views'. Why are views so sought after and enjoyed?

Main phase

Part 1

Read through with students the example on the worksheet entitled: 'What a view!'

Part 2

Ask students to imagine somewhere with a nice view and describe it in the style of the example.

Part 3

Ask students to swap work with each other and find one good part of the description and one area where it could be enhanced.

Plenary

Students to read their descriptions to the class and the class try to imagine the view. Students to discuss the images which came into their minds as the descriptions were being read.

Suggestions for homework

Students to find pictures of wonderful views, write a description, and then bring in the description and the picture.

Suggestions for development of this work

Arrange a wall display with pictures and highlights from the descriptions.

Extended exercise to develop a KS4 focus based on this work

Ask students to find descriptions of views from great literature and to study them to see how the adjectives are used. Remind them that great descriptions don't overuse adjectives. Ask students to highlight the parts of the descriptions they enjoyed.

Extended exercise to develop a KS5 focus based on this work

Arrange with local infants and junior schools an exercise where a picture of a nice view is described by a seven-year-old, a nine-year-old and an AS-level student at your own school. The students can then study the linguistic changes and developments in the use of skill in the language of the descriptions. They can then write a report of their findings.

What a view!

We had just reached the summit of the mountain in Scotland and had taken care to wait until we had reached the very top before we rewarded ourselves with the view. Now we were here. We swung round and took in the view. The four hours of climbing were suddenly worth every bit of effort. The sunshine was brilliant and the air was fresh and clear and still so that we could see to the furthest horizon. Sitting jagged in the distance on that horizon were the dark blue ranges of mountains and you could just see the snowy tops, their brilliant whiteness glaring with reflected sunshine. You found your eye picking up the end of the valley and following the loch through its twists and turns to the foot of the mountain you were now on. The water reflected the greys and blues of the sky and it was like another sky before you, silent and twisted and upside down. To the edges of the great expanse of water nestled clumps of brown and green forests, and here and there were clearings with broad patterns of shadows and earth colours in magical arrangements before us. A tiny boat was making its slow way to a little island in the loch. On that tiny island were clues of some ruined castle standing tiny and half-hidden among trees and bushes. There was a delight in sweeping your field of vision from the distance to the foreground and it seemed as if you could take in the whole sweep of the world. It made you feel small and insignificant but at the same time fascinated and awestruck at the scale of this landscape.

Describe the View　　　　　　　　　　　　　　　　　**WORKSHEET**

Key skills

1. Creating mood.
2. Writing to a theme.

Starter

Ask students to make a list and comment on times when they have looked forward to something.

Main phase

Discuss with students that sometimes things which are looked forward to do not always work out as anticipated.

Part 1

Read through with them Part 1 and discuss ideas about how it might continue. Point out that the atmosphere and mood can be enhanced by what is going on in the background of a scene. For example, when Richard was waiting in a happy mood the music was playing and he was relaxed. When Sophie arrived and seemed in a bad mood the music stopped and there was the unpleasant sound of the broken cups. These little background details amplify the feeling of the scene and help the reader identify and engage with the changes of mood.

Ask students to have a go at continuing the scene for a short while. Can they find ways of enhancing mood?

Part 2

Read through with the students the suggested scenarios and ask students to choose one and write it out, modelling it on the style of the example.

Plenary

Students to read their stories to each other in pairs.

Suggestions for homework

Ask students to chat the homework task over with their parents and guardians and family members. Ask them if they have had an experience where something which was looked forward to went wrong. Would they be happy to share it and allow it to be written up? Students to take key point notes and then write it up as a story.

Suggestions for development of this work

Students to research famous people to find out what their disappointments in life have been. They could set out their findings in an article written for a class magazine with the title: 'Famous Disappointments'.

Extended exercise to develop a KS4 focus based on this work

Ask students to write an essay in answer to this question: 'In what ways can disappointments strengthen the person?'

Extended exercise to develop a KS5 focus based on this work

Ask students to write two of any of the following about the subject of 'disappointment':

1. A play.
2. A poem.
3. A short story.
4. A mini play.

They are then to write an essay to answer this question: 'With reference to the two forms of writing you have chosen, explain how the experience of the reader differs when considering the subject of disappointment, depending on the form of expression used.'

Part 1

Background

Richard has met a girl called Sophie at a party, and they seemed to have hit it off very well. They have arranged to meet the next day at a cafe in the town at eleven O'Clock. From the moment Richard woke up, he had been pacing around excited about meeting what might be the new love of his life.

Richard and Sophie

He dressed in his best clothes and walked to the town with a spring in his step.

When he entered the cafe he quickly scanned round in case she had already arrived. Should he now just wait or should he sit with a drink and look cool and relaxed? He decided to go for the drink. He couldn't resist a muffin to go with it.

He strategically placed himself so that he could easily see the door. He stirred his coffee and went over the events of the previous evening in his mind. He felt relaxed and lulled by the soft, relaxing saxophone music of the cafe. He thought hard. It was Sophie who had suggested this meeting, wasn't it? He felt very lucky as he sat there. That smile of hers! That dress she wore! Wow!

Sophie arrived a few minutes after 11 and spotted Richard immediately. She came towards him bundled in a heavy coat, with no trace of a smile, and sat with him.

'What can I get you?' asked Richard as he rose from the table.

'Nothing, thanks. I've just had breakfast.'

'Oh.' There was an awkward pause. 'Nothing at all?' Richard enquired. He felt an odd lessening of his earlier excitement. He sat down and continued to eat his muffin. As he spoke, a few flurries of cake flew embarrassingly from his mouth.

'I had a great time last night. It was great meeting you . . . did you enjoy yourself?' He wiped the corners of his mouth with a tissue and looked at her.

Sophie looked at him hard and long. In the kitchen some cups were dropped and there was the sound of someone cursing. The song ceased and the sound of discordant chattering filled the room.

'Richard, it was sweet of you to meet me here, but er, I'm afraid I've got something to tell you.'

Part 2

Have a look at the following scenarios where anticipation of a nice event changes to an unpleasant experience.

Scenario and outline of the background	A suggested opening	Possible ideas about how the situation might develop
Waiting to meet a famous person who you have admired for years.	It had been two hours' wait but surely that was him over there walking this way. At last.	The famous person is distracted and walks away from you.
Meeting a friend from years ago.	The train pulled in and a sense of excitement surged through my body. After all these years . . .	The person has changed beyond all recognition . . .
You have won a dream holiday.	We arrived, not to the expected sunshine, but to torrential rain . . .	Everything that could go wrong, does go wrong . . .

The Disappointment　　　　　　　　　　　　　　　　　　**WORKSHEET**

Key skills

1. Writing poetry.

Starter

Ask students to refer to the starter on the worksheet and then write how they feel and what their immediate reactive thoughts are about each one (without pondering on it too much). The first one on the worksheet is done as an example.

Main phase

Part 1

Read through with the students the examples of the Impression Poems.

Point out and discuss the following aspects:

The poems are short and just provide little clues and hints and impressions in order to prompt and nudge the reader to reconstruct a bigger picture in the imagination.

Remind them to pause, just slightly, at the end of each line, when they read them out.

Part 2

Ask students to look at the Suggestion List and select one to write a poem about. Ask them to write a poem in response, using the brief style of the worked examples.

Plenary

Ask students to read out their poems to each other in pairs. Ask this listener to describe what came into their mind when they heard the poem.

Suggestions for homework

Ask students to come up with their own title and write an impression poem about it.

Suggestions for development of this work

Arrange for the class to copy out their own poem in best writing for a wall display. Get them to illustrate the images in the poems.

Extended exercise to develop a KS4 focus based on this work

Ask students to research and find ten technical terms used in poetry. Write them out and write definitions of them. Find examples of them in poems and write poems which use them.

Extended exercise to develop a KS5 focus based on this work

Obtain a copy of 'An Irish Airman Foresees His Death' by W. B. Yeats and 'The Love Song of Alfred J. Prufrock' by T. S. Eliot. Ask students to complete this task: 'Concentrating on rhythm and rhyme, compare the poems and write out your findings in detail.'

Starter list

1. A suit of armour. Thoughts and feelings might be:
   Danger, fighting and ghosts.
   Silver, polish, reflections.
   Castles, weapons, museums and ancestors.
2. Handshake.
3. Hairbrush.
4. Thermometer.

5. A bar of chocolate.
6. A coat with lots of pockets.
7. A clown.
8. A carnival.
9. A huge ball of string.
10. A cowboy.

Ask students to briefly discuss their responses with their partners.

Poems suggestion list

1. The postman on a frosty morning.
2. The factory in full swing with action and noise and people.
3. A board game where the players are having a great time.
4. A forest at night.
5. A zoo just after closing time.

6. The moon reflecting on the sea.
7. A river gushing in torrents of energy.
8. A mobile phone to be purchased in a shop window.
9. An invitation to a party, dropped through the letter box.
10. A travelling funfair being set up on the village green.

Examples of poems

A Bakery at Dawn

A faint yellow light; grey windows;
A stale musty, slightly choking, yeasty smell.
Sticky old dough underfoot;
Sad aprons hung on bronze hooks, bearing their smudged
    emblems of jam;
Tins of sugar on wooden shelves,
Blocks of confectionary chocolate wrapped in greaseproof
    paper,
Machines standing silently dusted gently with a thin veil of
    flour.
Look at the well-worn bench with the well-worn cloth,
And the oven, over there, its heavy iron door open, cold
    and waiting,
Yawning like a witch's toothless mouth,
Missing,
The heat of its fire.
Missing,
The smell of the crusty hot bread.
Something in here is . . .
Missing.

Covered Market at Dusk

Lights everywhere,
A huge looming dark sky,
A sense of 'Let's go home' everywhere,
Shivers, laughter, hunched shoulders;
Beads and jewellery, fruit and leather bags,
Second-hand books piled up here and scattered there;
Price stickers on the floor,
Vans with their doors wide open,
Boxes and grates hurriedly chucked in.
A man stands yawning,
A traffic warden rubs his hands together, with a sense of
weariness,
A little boy notices what none of the market traders have
noticed all day:
A nice little picture of Spain on a crate of oranges,
It must be time to go home.

Empty Deckchair

Yellow and red stripes.
The sound of the sea woven into its cloth texture,
The taste of the salt rubbed into its wood.
Cheap gaudy sunglasses hurriedly thrown down,
A fluffy white towel, half damp, half sandy, crumpled by the
    sandcastle, half built.
A cup of tea half drunk,
A magazine, discarded,
A bottle of suntan lotion, its awkward top screwed half on,
A postcard half written,
A pink stick of rock with its cellophane half off.
Where is she?

Feelings and Impressions Poetry **WORKSHEET**

Section H: Connections

Key skills
1. Writing in dialogue form.
2. Thinking creatively about connections.

Starter
Ask students to write down a list of different jobs.

Main phase

Part 1
Discuss how each job has its own particular tasks and skills. If you think creatively you can think about how almost any two jobs, which appear quite different at first, do in fact have certain things in common. Read through the dialogue in Part 1. Discuss what else this might have gone on to say.

Part 2
When they have written one dialogue, ask them to experiment with another pair of jobs. Ask them to use jobs from their own list made in the Starter, or any more they can think about.

Plenary
Arrange for students to read out, in role-play form, examples of the dialogues.

Suggestions for Homework
Ask students to research a wider range of jobs and write a more detailed dialogue between any two workers in those different jobs.

Suggestions for development of this work
Ask students to research a particular job in a lot of detail, finding out as much as they can about what that particular job actually involves. They may well wish to choose a job that they might one day wish to do. Ask them to bring in their research next lesson and stage a class discussion where the finer details of various jobs are presented by a randomly chosen pair of students, and then the rest of the group creatively suggest inventive ways in which the two jobs are connected. Then move on to the next random pair.

Extended exercise to develop a KS4 focus based on this work
Specialized vocabulary. Ask students to pick five jobs and research and write out a few examples of specialized vocabulary (words and phrase) specifically used for each job. Ask them to define and write down what each specialist word or phrase means.

Extended exercise to develop a KS5 focus based on this work
Ask students to look at the dialogue in the worked example of the conversation between the doctor and the postman. Imagine you are the doctor. You think about the conversation you had with the postman (which intrigues you) and come up with some more connections in your mind on the journey home. Write a letter to the postman explaining the further connections you have discovered. Then compare the letter to the dialogue and write a short report which compares the features of spontaneous speech (dialogue) with the more formal written letter.

Part 1

Imagine a doctor discussing her job with a postman. They are on a railway platform and the train has been delayed. They strike up a conversation:

Doctor: It's a shame the train is delayed. I can't wait to get home, it's been a difficult day.

Postman: I know what you mean. I was up at 4 this morning.

Doctor: Really. What do you do?

Postman: I'm a postman. What about you?

Doctor: Oh, I'm a doctor. I was having an interesting conversation with my partner last night. We discovered that all jobs are connected in some way.

Postman: How is my job connected to yours? You cure patients of illnesses and I stick letters through letterboxes!

Doctor: Yes, that's right. But think about it. If I have the important results of a medical test I send them to the patient. And who delivers them? You do!

Postman: I see. That is something to think about.

Part 2

Think of imaginary conversations between any two of the following pairs. See if, by writing a lively realistic dialogue, you can come up with a connection between the two jobs.

1. A teacher meets a farmer.
2. A dancer meets a shop assistant.
3. A fireman meets a vicar.
4. A gardener meets an inventor.

Job Connections   WORKSHEET

Key skills

1. Writing to explain.
2. Writing in dialogue form.

Starter

Read this out to the students: 'Have you ever wandered around a car boot sale, a jumble sale or a shop which sells second-hand goods and imagined the history of the items and how they got there?

Write a list of ten items which could possibly have an interesting, varied and well-travelled past, for example, book, coin, old framed picture, etc.

Jot down notes of what the history of the item might have been.

Main phase

1. Read 'The old candlestick holder' on the worksheet to the class.
   Discussion point: point out that the object can take on a personality matched to what it is.
2. Ask students to select from the suggestions and write a dialogue with an object in a suitable style.

Plenary

Read out, in pairs, the dialogues.

Suggestions for homework

Ask students to find an old object at home (or on the internet) and research its background. Write a more detailed dialogue with the object.

Suggestions for development of this work

Make a book with illustrations of the object on one page and the dialogue from the student typed out on the facing page. Try to include as many examples from the group as you can.

Extended exercise to develop a KS4 focus based on this work

Ask students to pick any two objects and write an extended and detailed dialogue between them where they tell each other stories of things which have happened to them.

Extended exercise to develop a KS5 focus based on this work

Ask students to imagine that they were an old, interesting object. Write out an interesting and detailed history of the object and then prepare a dramatic monologue to perform to the rest of the class.

Task 1

The old candlestick holder

As you are searching through an old drawer one day, you find an old candlestick holder. It is a small gold figure of a girl holding a container above her head in which many candles over the years have been placed.

The following takes place:

Me:	(Thinking aloud) I wonder if this old thing is valuable.
Gold Figure:	No, I'm afraid not. I might look gold but it's only gold plated I'm afraid.
Me:	You can speak? (Disbelief)
Gold Figure:	Yes, I can speak. What do you want to know? (Bored voice)
Me:	(Thinking hard) Well, tell me where and when were you made?
Gold Figure:	I was made in France in the 1950s. Paris if you must know. They turned me out by the thousand.
Me:	Then what happened?
Gold Figure:	Well, I was packaged up in a box and taken by lorry to a huge great warehouse where I was just dumped. I thought I'd be there for ever. Then one day I found myself popped onto the shelf of a shop window with bright lights shining on me. It wasn't long before a kind lady bought me for 15 francs and brought me here to England. By the way, that lady was Mary, your nan.
Me:	This is fascinating, really. Were you ever used?
Gold Figure:	Oh yes. For years I was used. Sometimes they put those cheap old candles in my holder but at Christmas they put the expensive nativity candles in; you know, the ones with marks to indicate the hours? They were great, those ones were. Then, after Christmas it was back to the old cheap candles again. Mind you, when there was a power cut I was important then, I can tell you.
Me:	Did they clean you?
Gold Figure:	Of course they cleaned me! Your mother used to polish me until I shined. I remember one evening while they were relaxing by the big old open fire, your mum looked across to me and she said: 'Look at the way the candlelight reflects on the gold. Isn't it heavenly!' That made me so feel good, so appreciated, I can tell you.
Me:	So how did you end up in this old drawer?
Gold Figure:	A few years ago they had a bit of a sort-out and I found myself chucked in this old drawer. I tell you what I miss the most – the light. I miss my candles, I do. You couldn't start using me again, could you?
Me:	Of course. I'll go and get a candle now. It'll be a cheap one I'm afraid, but at least you'll be used once again.
Gold Figure:	Thank you. That will mean a lot to me.

Task 2

Write a dialogue with an object in the style of the example above. Choose from the suggestions below and continue.

Object and scenario	Possible history	How the dialogue may start
A huge old oak table with carved wooden legs. Found on a visit to an old Norman castle.	Perhaps the table dates back to William the Conqueror. The table might remember great feasts with important people from history seated round.	Me: What a marvellous old table. Table: Thank you. I've been around a bit, and I've got a few stories, I could tell you. Me: Please tell me . . .
An old full-length mirror with a silver border mounted on a stand with small wheels. Your grandma has given it to you as a present.	Maybe it was given to your grandma, years ago, by a rich lady whom she used to work for in a rambling country house.	Me: When I buy a new set of clothes, it's great to be able to see them so well with this great mirror grandma gave me. Mirror: Yes, you look wonderful. I've seen a few sights in my life, I can tell you . . .
A set of heavy embroidered curtains purchased in an auction of the contents of an old house.	The curtains have been hanging in a big old lounge for many years. They have witnessed many events, but one which perhaps might stand out is when a burglar hid behind them.	Me: Goodness, you're heavy aren't you? (As you draw them for the night) Curtains: Yes I am. But that's how I keep the room so cosy and warm . . .
A Chinese hand-held fan with pictures of dragons on it. Purchased for a few pounds at a jumble sale.	Made in China and bought by a tourist. Perhaps it travelled around the world a bit before it ended up in the jumble sale.	Me: This is a lovely fan. So light and effective on such a hot day. Fan: I'm glad someone appreciates me. I've been to some pretty hot places you know . . .

Where Did You Come From? **WORKSHEET**

95

Key skills

1. Writing descriptively about a scene without action.
2. Placing action into the scene.

Starter

Write a list of places where a lot of people meet up together for various activities or events.

Main phase

Part 1

Read through with the students 'The icy river – frozen scene' and 'The icy river – action scene'.

Explain that the idea is to take a scene and describe it twice. The first description concentrates on the idea of stillness using words and phrases which reinforce the idea of stillness. The second description is the same scene, but this time with a dramatic action taking place in its midst. The feeling of action is evoked with the use of strong verbs. It is interesting to compare the reader's imaginative response to the same scene described in contrasting ways.

Part 2

Read through with the students the suggestions for contrasting scenes.

Ask them to write contrasting descriptions of the same scene when still and then when in action, in the style of the example.

Plenary

Ask selected students to read their contrasting descriptions to the class. Ask the class to comment on the ways in which the same scene is made to sound so different.

Suggestions for homework

Ask students to use the same method of writing contrasting descriptions at home. They can choose from the list of suggestions or perhaps come up with their own. They can spend more time planning it and writing in more detail.

Suggestions for development of this work

Extend the idea of contrasting descriptions to people. Ask students to describe someone at rest and when calm compared to when in action.

Extended exercise to develop a KS4 focus based on this work

Ask students to select a scene from a work of literature which they are currently studying on the course which contains either action or stillness. Ask them to write a contrasting scene. In other words, if the scene from the book is still and calm, the student is to write it out full of action, and vice versa.

Extended exercise to develop a KS5 focus based on this work

Students to carry out the exercise described in the KS4 Focus and in addition write an essay to answer this question: 'When we see a character in fiction still and quiet, we learn very little about her. When she is in action, we learn a lot. Do you agree? Illustrate your answer with examples from one of the books you are studying.'

Part 1

The icy river – frozen scene

The ice was sitting in patches on the surface of the water. The water itself was a deep blue-and-black mixture. The patches of ice were like phantom white and grey water lilies. The night was still and the air hung like a frozen cloak. By the side of the river the trees bent over the bank with the silent strain of the snowfall. They seemed like a row of monks fishing in quiet shadows. Icicles formed intricate gothic patterns between the weeds and undergrowth. There were no footprints in the heavy thick snow. No traces of animal movement. Nothing moved. The dome of dark blue and black above stretched infinitely into deeper blues and deeper blacks. The air itself seemed to hang solidly there, not waiting; just being. Everything was frozen; everything was still. And the stillness and the silence held each other in an icy embrace.

The icy river – action scene

The shouting seemed to echo around the frozen trees. Along the river came a small rowing boat. A police officer, in the boat, wearing a yellow reflective jacket was shining his torch into the undergrowth and shouting for someone. A flustered man in a heavy black coat pulled on the oars. Muffled rustlings could be heard here and there by the sides of the river as rabbits scurried off from the noise. The torch was shone up into a tree and the snow sparkled in the sweeping beam of light, and then as the beam swung round, the branch returned to lurking shadows and dimness. The oars of the boat were furiously thumped into the icy water, sometimes entering straight into water; sometimes smacking the hard patches of ice. The bow of the boat scrapped its way forward. The shouting and the frantic searching continued.

Part 2

Suggestions for contrasting scenes

1. The farm
Describe a farm at night. Think about the large barns, the haystacks, the tractors and farm machinery standing still and silent, perhaps in silvery moonlight. Then imagine the farm in mid-morning on a summer's day. Tractors working the fields, animals being fed and herded, perhaps a threshing machine in full swing.

2. The pop concert
Describe a concert venue before anyone arrives. Then describe the venue when it is in full swing at the concert.

3. The football match
Describe the stadium first thing in the morning before anyone arrives. Then describe the stadium when the match is under way.

Descriptions: Frozen Scene and Action **WORKSHEET**

Key skills

1. Description skills.
2. Experimenting with a method for writing a description.

Starter

Provide a variety of pictures for the class (or project one onto the board) and ask the students to spend a few minutes describing it in writing.

Main phase

Provide the students with a set of pictures. These can be photographs from a magazine or reproductions of great paintings.

The student studies the picture and writes a description looking at the style of the example description (in Part 1) and using the checklist on the worksheet (Part 2).

The student then reads the description to the class who imagine what the picture looks like.

The picture is then shown to the class (ideally on an OHT) and the class comment on how it compares to their imaginative picture in their mind's eye.

Plenary

Students to make their own list of what is required to write a good description of a picture.

Suggestions for homework

Students to find their own picture and write a description of it using the checklist and again looking at the style of the example description.

Suggestions for development of this work

Arrange a workshop session where pictures are described and then suggestions made by the students as to how the written description could be improved and enhanced. Encourage a session of experimentation.

Extended exercise to develop a KS4 focus based on this work

Students to find, guided by the teacher, descriptions of places and people from literature and copy out a selection of descriptions. They then experiment and draw the scenes, or people, based on their reading of the written descriptions. This will help them to pay close attention to the way writers create their descriptive effects.

Extended exercise to develop a KS5 focus based on this work

Students to carry out the same exercise as the KS4 focus exercise above. In addition, they find examples of poetry which describe people and places. They then experiment with creating pictures in response to both prose descriptions and poetic descriptions. Once they have carried out these exercises, they write an essay in response to this question: 'How does poetry differ from prose writing in its power to create descriptive effects?'

Part 1

An example of a written description of a great painting

'Actors of the Comedie Italienne' (c. 1718) by the artist Antoine Watteau.

The dominant colours of the picture are rich browns and yellowy browns. There are a group of people gathered around a man who is playing what appears to be an old-fashioned guitar. Another man, to his side, holds a giant burning torch, which gives off a strong yellow light and casts a warm glow onto the faces and bodies of the assembled small group.

As you look into the background of the picture you see deep, dark shadows where the light hasn't reached. There is a strong contrast between the dark background and the warmly lit foreground. The atmosphere created is one of warmth and comfort. It is clear that the painting is very old from the style of the clothing with neck ruffs and silken garments. There is a strong sense of wealth here.

From the look on the faces of the gathered people, they are enjoying the moment and are very interested in the musician. There is a feeling of peace and enjoyment. In the full glare of the light, just set back a little from the man holding the burning torch is a strange looking man. He is dressed as a harlequin and holds his arm up in a dramatic gesture. As you examine the picture more closely, you become aware that some sort of performance is being carried out here. Maybe they are a group of travelling entertainers. To the right is a man leaning forward on his walking-stick and watching intensely. Just disappearing into the shadows beyond is a small black-and-white dog, which, judging by its body language, is ready to go home. To the left is a young girl holding a dim lamp amd leaning in to glimpse the performance. Heads dotted about, some half in shadow, are leaning here and there to look in. The artist has caught a very special moment in time charged with a sense of drama.

Part 2

Checklist for describing a picture:

1. Are there colours? How many? Is there a dominant colour?
2. Are there people? What attitude do they show? What body language? What type of clothes are they wearing? What are they doing?
3. What is the atmosphere or mood created in the picture?
4. What time of day do you think it is?
5. What time of the year?
6. Is it set inside or outside?
7. What objects are in the picture?
8. Does the picture tell a story? If so, what is the story?
9. Is there anything unusual or mysterious about the picture?
10. Describe how the lighting works in the picture. What about the shadows?
11. Is there anything which stands out in the picture?
12. What is in the foreground, the background, the middle ground?
13. Is there action or movement depicted in the picture?
14. What types of materials or textures are there?
15. Where does your eye get drawn to? Is there a focal point?
16. Are there buildings?
17. Are there any methods of transport shown?
18. Are there plants?
19. How does the picture make you feel?

Describe a Picture — **WORKSHEET**

Key skills

1. Writing from a distinct viewpoint.
2. Understanding character.

Starter

Imagine that grandparents took their grandchildren to a theme park for a special day out. Make notes on how the experiences would be different for the teenage children compared to the grandparents.

Main phase

Part 1

Explain to the students that this exercise is designed to show that people experience events in accordance with their own particular view of the world. It is usually what they are interested in which they notice and focus on. For example, somebody who cuts hair for a living, when meeting you, will immediately notice your hair. The exercise helps when writing about character and making characters in fiction become more alive and believable.

Read through Part 1 one of the worksheet and discuss. See if any other characters come to mind and discuss what their impressions of the evening might be.

Part 2

Read through the example scenarios and the suggested characters and ask them to write their own brief impressions of an experience in the style of the worked example in Part 1. The characters and scenarios can be 'mixed and matched'.

Plenary

Read to each other, in pairs, a variety of brief impression viewpoints from the work done.

Suggestions for homework

Ask students to choose a scenario and a selection of characters from Part 2 of the worksheet. This is to be one they haven't yet worked on in the class. They are then to sketch out the scene and draw in the characters and add speech bubbles to explain the various characters' brief viewpoint impressions. Students may wish to cut and stick suitably appropriate pictures from magazines and produce a mixed sketch and collage presentation.

Suggestions for development of this work

Ask students to think up a scenario themselves and place a variety of celebrity and famous people (who they admire) into the imaginative scene. They can then write out brief viewpoint impressions from the viewpoints of the famous people.

Extended exercise to develop a KS4 focus based on this work

Students to take a scene from a work of literature which they have been studying and assemble imaginatively characters from the book. They are then to write out brief viewpoint impressions from the point of view of the characters in the style of the worked example but also using their knowledge of the characters.

Extended exercise to develop a KS5 focus based on this work

Students to carry out the exercise described in the KS4 Focus exercise above. They are then to carry out this exercise: 'Imagine that the author of your book had a conversation with one of the characters. The character asks the author why he has been created in the way he has. Write out, in dialogue form, the conversation which would then take place.'

Part 1

Scenario 1: Ten-pin bowling

Imagine the cross-section of people that might be found at a ten-pin bowling alley on a particular evening. Afterwards, a few were chosen and asked about their experience. Here are some brief impressions which they gave:

Melanie, a teenage girl, aged 14: 'I loved the music and the music video on the screens everywhere. It was good to see the up-to-date fashions. The atmosphere was vibrant and exciting.'

Gavin, a college art student, aged 19: 'When they put the lights really dim with just the bowling alleys lit up, I got an idea for a work of art. I'm going to put thousands of tiny little bulbs in a curly pattern on a piece of board and set it up so that a pink light travels around and reverses direction. I think that would look really good.'

Allan, a retired man, aged 60: 'I love to play for a couple of hours here once a week. I find that being retired makes the time go slowly and I need something to occupy my mind. The coffee they serve here is particularly good.'

Susie, a child of six. 'The jelly beans are lovely. They are all different colours.'

Martin, a 30-year-old businessman: 'I've noticed how busy the place always is and I'm thinking of setting up a bowling alley business myself.'

Margaret, a woman of 47 who does part-time cleaning for a living: 'I noticed all the chewing gum trodden into the carpet here. It is a shame because it is a lovely quality carpet.'

Barry, a trainee chef, aged 20: 'That hot dog I just had was great. I didn't think a sausage could taste so good. It tasted as if it was barbecued. Very nice.'

Part 2

Suggested scenarios:

1. Wandering around a little town set on a hill by the Mediterranean Sea.
2. Taking a taxi ride through London on a day when the rain is lashing down.
3. Staying in a log cabin high up in the Alps.
4. Wandering around New York City.
5. Camping in a forest.
6. Watching a huge and colourful carnival procession.
7. Taking a tour around a factory which makes toys.
8. Buying something in the world's biggest sweet shop.
9. Walking around a new art gallery.
10. Being stranded on a coach trip in Scotland with a thick fog shrouding everything.

Suggested characters who can give their brief viewpoint impressions of the experience:

1. A young child.
2. A woman of twenty who runs her own successful business.
3. A retired man.
4. A carpenter aged 30.
5. A woman of 40 who works at a zoo.
6. A young police officer.
7. A soldier who won a medal for bravery.
8. A fireman.
9. A nurse.
10. A schoolteacher.

Character Viewpoints　　　　　　　　　　　　　　　　**WORKSHEET**

Key skills

1. Writing to persuade, argue and explain.

Starter

Write down for a few moments why we compare ourselves to others. Discuss in the class the findings.

Main phase

Part 1

Read through with the class the examples. Explain that each presents their side of the argument.

Part 2

Ask students to choose one of the suggestions and write out a conversation in the style of the examples in Part 1 of the worksheet.

Plenary

Students to read out in pairs one of the conversations. Discuss whether both arguments are presented.

Suggestions for homework

Students to find their own 'pair' to write a conversation in the style of the examples.

Suggestions for development of this work

Students to write an essay on this subject: 'Money is all that matters in life'. They are to include arguments for and against the statement.

Extended exercise to develop a KS4 focus based on this work

Students to write a detailed essay on this subject: 'Prisons are not the most effective form of punishment'. They are to include arguments for and against the statement.

Extended exercise to develop a KS5 focus based on this work

Students to research and then write a detailed essay on this subject: 'Art is really not much use in the world'. They are to include arguments for and against the statement.

Part 1

1. Water compared to milk

Water: I'm better than you. Nothing quenches the thirst better than me.

Milk: That may well be true, but in the morning people can't pour just water over their cereal, can they? That's where I come in. There's nothing quite like milk.

Water: Wait a moment. Think about it. Without me, there would be no oceans, no rivers, no clouds. In fact, there would be no life at all, that's how important I am!

Milk: Not so fast. You are forgetting about little babies. Without me what would we give little babies? They must have milk. They wouldn't do so well on just water, would they? The future of the human race depends on little babies getting milk.

2. The magpie and the hedgehog

Magpie: I'm better than you in so many ways. I can fly and look at the whole world from above and decide where to go. All you can do is snort around at night and muddle aimlessly about.

Hedgehog: Just one moment, Mr Magpie. What about if you get attacked? You've got no defence system, have you? Well, I have. Who's going to try to sink their teeth into me with all these spikes? Eh?

3. The play at the theatre and the movie

Movie: Who goes to see you any more? You're so old-fashioned! OK, so once people liked to go to the theatre, they had nothing else; Shakespeare and all that! But now they need action-packed thrills and cutting-edge technology. With the way special effects are today, nobody is going to sit in a theatre watching a bunch of people talking on a stage! How boring is that?

Theatre: You forget that we theatre plays offer something that you movies could never provide.

Movie: And what exactly is that?

Theatre: The atmosphere of live theatre. What the audience see and hear is exactly as it happens. They are part of it. The reaction of the audience affects the actors on the stage. There is a sort of communication between the two. Your movies, on the other hand, are cut and edited and changed and have special effects added. You're so far removed from the original action, it's unbelievable.

Movie: But we are more entertaining.

Theatre: Surely that is a matter of opinion. If we theatres are so old-fashioned and out of touch, how do you explain that there are thousands of us putting plays on all the time all over the world?

Movie: OK, fair enough. You are, perhaps, not finished off quite yet.

Part 2

Suggestions for comparison conversations

1. The train is more important than the railway station.
2. The cup is better than the saucer.
3. Plastic is better than wood.
4. Walking is better than cycling.
5. A pen is better than a pencil.
6. Hot weather is better than cold.
7. Boots are better than shoes.
8. Red is nicer than blue.

Let's Argue Our Case **WORKSHEET**

Key skills

1. Writing character descriptions.

Starter

Word association: ask students to write out the following ten words and write down which character and place they would instinctively connect to them:

1. Road sign.
2. Darkness.
3. Shoe polish.
4. Cinema.
5. Skateboard.
6. Darts board.
7. Bus.
8. White robe.
9. DNA.
10. Jewellery.

Main phase

Part 1

Explain to students that a word or phrase is taken and used as a 'connection' to be used by a range of characters in a variety of situations. These will show a mini scenario and the essence of a character.

Read through, with students, the worked example for the word 'stones' and discuss.

Part 2

Read through the suggested words list, the character list and the situations. Ask students to try connecting the key words with the characters and situations at random to sharpen their imaginative connecting skills. See worked examples on the worksheet where a random key word has been connected to the first three characters and the first three situations.

Plenary

Ask students to read out examples to the class.

Suggestions for homework

Students to take home a copy of the lists and have a go at writing some more connected situations in mini scenario form.

Suggestions for development of this work

Students to choose their best mini scenario and then develop it into a longer, more detailed story.

Extended exercise to develop a KS4 focus based on this work

Students to work in groups and create their own lists of key words, characters and scenarios. As a group, see how many mini scenarios they can write collaboratively using the style and method as set out in Part 1 of the worksheet.

Extended exercise to develop a KS5 focus based on this work

Arrange for students to work in groups and see who can create the best educational board game based on the Character Connections idea. They must show their designs and write out clear instructions on how to play. They must identify and define their audience. A report must then be written to explain how the game will help the word skills of the players.

Part 1

Take the word 'stones'. How many characters and situations can you think of where this word could be used in a situation to reveal an aspect of character?

Worked example:

1. 'Can I take some of these <u>stones</u> home, Mummy?' A young child at the seaside.
2. 'Yer man, I love the <u>Stones</u>, the Beatles and the Bee Gees . . .' A hippy thinking back to the music of the sixties.
3. 'Ladies and Gentlemen, we now proudly announce our next item for auction. A series of exquisite precious <u>stones</u> set in a silver tiara. May I start the bidding at £1,000 . . .' An auctioneer at an auction house.
4. 'Let us remain quiet for a while and consider how acts of kindness and friendship shown to us can be compared to stepping stones on the journey across the river of life.' A vicar giving a sermon to his congregation.
5. 'Stash the <u>stones</u> Bernie, look, the police are coming down the drive . . .' One burglar talking to another.
6. 'These grave<u>stones</u> of the First World War soldiers stretch away into the distance as far as the eye can see and makes us all feel very sad.' A TV presenter on Remembrance Sunday.

Part 2

Look at the following lists of key words, characters and situations. Choose a key word and try to connect it to three characters in three different situations.

Key words and phrases

1. Sport.	11. Party.
2. Walk.	12. Roof.
3. Chase.	13. Silence.
4. Music.	14. Animal.
5. Snow.	15. Tourist.
6. Mountain.	16. Weather.
7. Shadow.	17. Excitement.
8. Glisten.	18. Flowers.
9. Phone.	19. Hour.
10. Wood.	20. Smoke.

List of characters

1. An old farmer.	6. A very sharp-eyed night watchman.
2. A young jockey.	7. A person who is obsessed with collecting things.
3. A weary traveller.	8. A private detective.
4. A milkman one day from retirement.	9. A happy and relaxed holidaymaker.
5. An impolite waiter.	10. A very clumsy person.

List of situations

1. A visit to the zoo.	6. On a bus late at night.
2. A tour of a lighthouse on a barren stretch of rocky coastline.	7. A fire engine on an emergency call-out.
3. A crowd flooding out of a football stadium after a big match.	8. A window cleaner up a high ladder.
4. Very early in the morning in a town.	9. A group of elderly people looking at some cute white puppies.
5. An amusement arcade at a holiday camp.	10. A group of monks visiting Stonehenge.

Examples

Key word: 'party' connected to Characters 1, 2 and 3 and situations 8, 9 and 10.

1. 'It reminds me of my youth on the farm. Feeding the animals and making sure they got well looked after was more fun for me than going to a <u>party</u>, I can tell you.'

An old farmer, who has taken his grandchildren to the zoo, is watching the zoo animals being fed and remembering when he first started work, years before.

2. 'It's nice to get away from it all and experience the peace of this place. Look, now that we're at the top of this lonely lighthouse we can see for miles along the rugged rocky coastline. It's nice to have a change. Working as a successful jockey you seem to go to a <u>party</u> every night and I'm a bit tired of all that and glad to have this break.' A jockey taking a few days' break and chatting with his friend.

3. A weary traveller is walking past a football stadium when suddenly the doors are flung open, the big match is over, and hundreds of supporters flood out. The traveller had been lost in thought but now sees a huge crowd hurrying towards him. 'Welcome to the <u>party</u>!' he thinks.

Character Connections **WORKSHEET**

Key skills

1. Travel diary writing.
2. Working collectively as a whole group.

The activity can be tailored to match all abilities, and the great thing is that at the end it is the whole journey that is important, with every class member playing their part. Some entries will be long and developed, others will be short and to the point. When they are all linked together, there will be rich variety.

Starter

Ask the students to make a list of as many different methods of transport as they can think of. From the class's contributions produce a master list.

Main phase

Preparation

Obtain a map of the world and divide it up into segments. Number the segments to match the number participating in the class. Display the map prominently.

Part 1

The students are to choose a section of the journey and an appropriate method of transport. For example, section 14 might be a stretch through the Sahara Desert. The selected means of transport may be a camel. That student now has to write out a description, in the form of a travel diary, of her part of the journey. Depending on the amount of time available, it would be helpful if the students are allowed some research time to read up on the situation in their chosen part of the world, and this will make their diary entry sound more authentic.

From an organizational point of view, you can keep a record of who covers which segment of the journey. A worked example is given in the worksheet, together with a set of suggestions for other parts of the journey.

Part 2

A student checklist is included to help the students with ideas when they come to write their own segment.

Plenary

Students to report on their progress so far this lesson.

Suggestions for homework

Ask students to produce an illustration for their part of the journey.

Suggestions for development of this work

When all the segments are in, they can be compiled, in the correct geographical order, into a class booklet. Illustrations, which were set for homework, can be included to bring to life the diverse nature of the long journey. Another outcome which this activity lends itself to is the production of a diverse and fascinating-looking wall display.

Extended exercise to develop a KS4 focus based on this work

With reference to the finished work of the class, students can choose a destination and write a developed and detailed answer to this: 'Write about an experience which you have had in another country.'

Extended exercise to develop a KS5 focus based on this work

Ask students to a variety of travel writing and write an essay in answer to this question:

'What are the characteristics of good travel writing? Illustrate your answer with examples from your research.'

Part 1

Example of a segment

Segment 14. The trip across the Sahara Desert.

For this next part of the journey, I got to travel on a camel as part of a camel caravan. Our guides were people who had lived in the desert all their lives. The plan was to travel at night as it was far too hot to travel during the day. This night we set off and in the sky I saw the stars as bright and clear as I had ever seen them. I could feel the rhythmic plod, plod of the camel's pace. It seemed to have one steady slow pace and it kept to that all the time. I was rocked about in a rhythmic way, hearing the strange snorts from the beast. Ahead of me I could see the faint yellow glow of the lanterns, one for each camel. In the still, chilly desert air I could hear the guides occasionally talking. Eventually, after many hours we stopped and made our camp. There we slept, but after only an hour the sun arose and the main problem for the day was staying cool. Tonight we continue our journey.

Part 2

Checklist for your segment of the journey:

1. Put a clear sub-heading to identify where you are.
2. Explain the method of transport clearly.
3. Include a description of a specific thing to help the reader imagine the scene. Remember to use all the senses (if possible).
4. Try to include some aspect which is particular to that part of the world.

Possible places to include and things to mention:

1. New York. Perhaps in a yellow taxi. What would the traffic, noise and rush be like?
2. Mid-west of America, perhaps by train. How would the view from the window be? Enormous sweeping fields? Mountains in the distance? What are the passengers on the train like?
3. Amazon rainforest. Perhaps you travel by canoe for this part of your journey? What colour is the water? How does it swirl? What do the edges of the thick forests look like? What wildlife is there?
4. Maybe the trip across the Pacific Ocean is as a passenger on a huge cargo ship. How does it feel with the enormous sway of the ocean? What is the food like? How do you feel?
5. Maybe you stop off at Easter Island in the middle of the vast ocean. You have a chance to see the mysterious carved heads. What thoughts run through your mind as you look at them and realize how enormous they are? What time of the day is it? How is the weather at this point?

Section I: Character

Key skills

1. Writing about character.

Starter

Ask students to think about an interesting person they know. It may be someone they know, or an acquaintance or somebody they may have seen on television. In just a few minutes ask them to describe that character.

Hear a few read out and discuss the sorts of information which go into a character description.

Ask them to make a list of the categories of information.

Main phase

Part 1

Read through with them Part 1.

Part 2

Read through with students and ask them to start to work on their own character description.

Plenary

Students to read out examples of their character descriptions. Students to help each other by suggesting which parts of the description are good and how certain other areas could perhaps be enhanced.

Suggestions for homework

Ask students to write two character descriptions using the style of the work used in class. Ask them to make their characters very different from each other. It is a good idea to put them together into an imaginary situation.

Suggestions for development of this work

Students to read each other's character descriptions and then choose three. They are then to write a short story which connects, links and features all three.

Extended exercise to develop a KS4 focus based on this work

Ask students to work in small groups and prepare a short talk to the class which explains how character can be described by having the character do something. They are to use examples from their own work to support their presentation.

Extended exercise to develop a KS5 focus based on this work

Ask students to choose five very different characters from the range produced by the class. They are then to write out an imaginary situation where the five characters meet and discuss a problem. The situation they are in becomes increasingly more dangerous. (Maybe they are trapped in a lift, for example.) Their characters are revealed through what they say and how they behave in response to the situation. The form should be a radio play. After the finished play, students are to write an answer to this question: 'Do you agree that the truth about a character is revealed in times of trouble? Support your answer with examples from your play.'

Part 1

A typical question about character is like this: 'Describe an interesting character and explain why he/she is interesting.'
In order to learn how to write about character, it is a good idea to put your character into an interesting and convincing situation and then describe him doing something. This captivates interest. The physical descriptions should not stand alone but should be given as the character is gradually revealed, through the action, to the reader.
For example, read about this character who runs a newsagents:

Good News Newsagents

One day, it must have been late winter, it was dark at five in the afternoon and I thought that his shop called 'Good News' was closed because it was dark inside. But as I approached the door I noticed that the tatty sign read 'Open'. I pushed open the door and a bell jingled somewhere in a back room. Mr Simpkins emerged from the gloom holding a candle which cast an eerie glow.

'Sorry about this,' he said as he shuffled up to the counter. 'I forgot to pay the electric. What can I do for you?' Surrounding him and gushing from the back room was an overpowering stench of boiled cabbage and he was wiping gravy from his mouth. His shirt was open at the top and a mass of grey chest hair nestled there, horribly.

'I just want an evening paper and a bar of chocolate please,' I said. The man held the candle over the papers on the counter and I could see huge bulging eyes straining to read the names of them. He picked one up after much licking of the thumb and rolled it up into a tight tube. This annoyed me as it made the paper hard to read and was totally unnecessary.

He selected a bar of chocolate from the display and held it out to me.

'Here you go, the sell-by's just gone but you can have that cheap,' he said. I didn't have the heart to tell him I'd rather pay full price for a bar of chocolate which is well within its sell-by date. I paid him the money and he cursed in quite an alarming way as he tried to bang the till to open it.

'Won't open without the electric,' he said. 'Can I give you yer change when you're next in?' I hesitated because I had handed him a £10 note and the cost of my paper and chocolate was a mere £1.20. I also remembered that, not that long ago, he had forgotten to give me my change the 'next time I was in' and then I didn't have the heart to mention it. I paused awkwardly.

He looked across at me, eyes bulging, face expressionless.

'Ok, that'll be fine. I'll see you tomorrow, then.' He seemed relieved and let out a bit of a sigh.

Part 2

Choose from the following and write about an imaginary meeting you have with the character where the character traits are revealed through the action.

Character	Character traits	Situation	Your involvement
Bus driver.	Always talking. Always cheerful. Tries to be funny all the time.	Bus breaks down in the countryside in the snow. Driver tries to entertain everyone while they wait for rescue. Doesn't go well.	A passenger in a hurry.
A holiday rep.	Grumpy. Unhelpful. Sarcastic. Moody.	A Spanish resort. The rep. is trying to get a group of you to sign up for an expensive holiday coach trip. He is very, very insistent.	You are a holidaymaker and your money is running out fast.
An eccentric character who, every day, voluntarily picks up rubbish in the street.	Sings loudly. Dresses strangely. Seems to be in her own little world.	She has fallen over outside your house and hurt herself.	You run to help her.

An Interesting Character **WORKSHEET**

Key skills

1. Writing about their own character.
2. Exploring symbols.

Starter

Ask students to list as many famous statues as they can and answer this question: 'What is the purpose of a statue?'

Main phase

Part 1

Read through Part 1 of the worksheet and ask them to start jotting down notes in preparation for their own statue design.

Part 2

Ask them to now write up in detail a design plan for their own statue.

Plenary

Ask students to read and look out for particularly interesting parts, in each other's work.

Suggestions for homework

Ask students to research and find a famous and interesting statue. They are to produce an information leaflet about the statue, to include an illustration, based on their research, but written out in their own words.

Suggestions for development of this work

Ask students to choose a partner. They then write out a specification for each other but don't show each other until it is finished.

Extended exercise to develop a KS4 focus based on this work

Students to swap each other's work and read in detail the design plan. They are then to imagine that the statue has been built. They go to visit it and write a detailed description of what they see.

Extended exercise to develop a KS5 focus based on this work

Explain to students that these statue designs involve the idea of symbols, where one thing is seen to represent something else. Ask students and guide them in finding examples of literature which use symbols and ask them to write an essay answering this: 'Give examples of how symbols have been used in literature.'

You have the opportunity for a famous sculptor to produce a statue of yourself. You have been asked to write out a specification:

Think about:

1. Pose.
2. Material.
3. Colour.
4. Size.

First of all, which pose should it be in? The pose must be one that is a representative symbol of the typical you.

Should it be: a fighter; a sleeper; a runner; a dancer?

Second, think about the material you would like your statue to be made from.

Should it be heavy, dark, expensive wood to represent quality? Or perhaps cardboard to show that you are a light and easy-going person?

Rubber to illustrate that you are flexible and often change your mind?

Now think about the colour.

Perhaps blue to show a relaxed calm personality?

Red to show that you get angry quickly?

White to show that at heart you are a peacemaker?

Yellow to show that you are a timid type of person?

Now, what about the size of your statue?

Small and dainty to be a small ornament to put on a shelf? Maybe you are not someone who likes to be noticed?

Or maybe a lifesize statue to illustrate your large-as-life personality?

So, describe each part in detail and explain why you have made the choices you have made.

Key skills

1. Writing about character.
2. Writing dialogue.

Starter

It is a fact of life that people who know you talk about you in your absence.

Ask students to imagine that someone who knows them was saying nice things about them in their absence. Now ask them to write down what they think would be said.

Now ask them to imagine that someone who knows them was saying not-so-nice things about them in their absence. Again, ask them to write down what they think would be said.

Main phase

Part 1

Read through the conversation entitled: 'We're going to miss him' on the worksheet. Discuss this with them. Point out that as information about the absent character is mentioned, a mental image starts to form itself in the imagination of the reader, little by little. The reason that the reader becomes interested in him is because the people discussing him are interested in him. Also, by discussing specific events and saying what the character did, it engenders a real, believable person.

Part 2

Ask students to have a go at writing out a conversation between friends who are discussing another friend who, for one reason or another, has become absent from them. Ask them to use a similar style to the example shown. They may say nice things about the person, or they may criticize him.

Remind students of the technique of giving little clues about the character, little by little. This allows an intriguing mental image to be gradually built up.

Plenary

Ask students to read out some of the conversations using different voices for the characters. Discuss them, highlighting good parts and areas where improvements could be made.

Suggestions for homework

Students to think about their favourite TV drama programme and choose three characters who remain, and a third, who for some imaginary reason becomes absent for a while. Write out a dialogue in the style of the worksheet where the characters discuss their absent friend.

Suggestions for development of this work

Ask students to think about and write in response to this: Imagine someone who is close to you goes away on a year-long trip to somewhere. Someone who knows you, but doesn't know the person who has gone away, asks you what that person is like. Write a detailed reply.

Extended exercise to develop a KS4 focus based on this work

Ask students to do this task: Think of a person in history who you admire. Prepare some research on that person and find out as much as you can about him/her. Now imagine that that person is miraculously transported through time to the present day and comes to live as your neighbour. Write out an imaginary dialogue between neighbours where the person's character is gradually revealed.

Extended exercise to develop a KS5 focus based on this work

Ask students to do this task: Find a work of literature which you like or would like to explore. Read and study it carefully (it can be one on your reading list). Choose two characters in the book who have a conversation about a third character in the book. Write out the conversation using the dialogue style based on the example on the worksheet.

Part 1
We're going to miss him

Situation: friends sit and discuss an absent friend.

Joanne: We'll miss him.

Sean: Yes, we will.

Gavin: He might not like it over there. Australia is all very well, but it's not for everyone, you know. He'll get homesick I bet. Thousands come home after a while.

Joanne: I don't think so. I don't think we must build up our hopes like that.

Sean: All we can do is remember the good times.

Gavin: Don't be like that. There is something else we can do.

Sean and Joanne: What?

Gavin: Start saving like mad for our airfares so we can go over and see him.

(Silence for a few moments)

Joanne: He'll probably meet a lovely Australian girl, fall in love, get married, have children and stay over there for ever.

Sean: You know how to cheer someone up, don't you?

Gavin: She's kidding.

Joanne: Am I?

Sean: Why did he have to go? Why did he reject his friends?

Joanne: Don't be so silly. He didn't reject his friends. His parents decided to emigrate to Australia and naturally they took their son with them.

Sean: But he didn't have to go.

Gavin: Look here, it's no use talking like this. The fact is he has gone and there's nothing we can do about it.

(Silent thought for a few moments)

Sean: Do you remember when he protected me from that rough gang in the park?

Gavin: How could we forget? They ran like hell.

Joanne: So would you if a guy that big came towards you.

Sean: Good job they didn't know he was a black belt in Judo. They'd have run even faster.

Joanne: I always wondered why he took up Judo. You know, being that big and everything.

Gavin: There were a lot of things I wondered about with Chris.

Joanne: Like what?

Gavin: Like how he managed to lay his hands on so much money all the time. You know, and buy us treats and everything.

Sean: He had loads of part-time jobs didn't he? And he used to buy things from second-hand shops, do them up and sell them on the internet.

Joanne: The thing I'll never forget is how good-looking he was.

Gavin: And how smart he dressed . . .

Sean: And how kind he was . . .

Joanne: And how he made you feel . . .

Gavin: What?

Joanne: You know . . . important. He made you feel important just by talking to you.

Gavin: We're going to miss him.

Key skills

1. Writing and revealing character in dialogue form.
2. Telling a story in an interesting way.

Starter

Ask students to describe what they have done so far today in two ways: narrative and dialogue.

Main phase

Part 1
Read through with students the story on the worksheet.

Part 2
Ask students to write a story using one of the opening lines on the suggestion list in the style of the example where a heavy reliance is placed on dialogue.

Plenary

Ask a few of the students to read their stories out to the class. If possible, arrange it so that different voices are used to read the dialogue.

Suggestions for homework

Ask students to take home their dialogue story and to try to rewrite it in the form mainly of narration.

Suggestions for development of this work

Students to produce a collage on a large sheet of paper with pictures cut out of various sources and pasted on. For each character, a speech bubble is written which matches their character.

Extended exercise to develop a KS4 focus based on this work

Students to select a small extract from one of the books they are studying on the course which includes some dialogue. They are then to rewrite it in the form mainly of narration.

Extended exercise to develop a KS5 focus based on this work

Students to carry out the exercise in the KS4 Focus and then write an answer to this question: 'How does the experience of the reader change when reading dialogue compared to reading narration?'

Part 1

Steven the railway crossing man

I used to go for a bike-ride down to the coast, every day in the summer holidays. My route used to take me across a railway line. The gates were opened and closed by a man known as Steven. It was when I had to wait for the train to pass that I would say Hello and get into minor conversation with Steven. One day he told me a fascinating story. It went like this:

'When you get to the T-junction, at the end of the lane ahead, do you turn left or right?' he asked.

'Usually right,' I said. 'I head for the sea front.'

'Well then, you go past Melvin's place.'

'Where is Melvin's place?' I asked.

'It's that huge old house, set back from the lane, with ivy on the walls.' As he said this he lent forward a little, as if he was going to tell me a secret. In fact, he turned his head, with its tufts of ginger hair, to check that nobody was listening in. There was a pause and he looked at me but I could see that his mind was elsewhere.

'What about it?' I asked.

'Melvin does magic,' he said.

'What, like card tricks and things?'

'No, not at all like card tricks.' Steven's expression darkened a little. 'Nothing at all like card tricks. And I know it's true what he can do, because I've seen it!'

'What can he do?' I asked, starting to become intrigued.

'Well, one evening, as I was walking home, 'cause I go past that place on the way home you see, I peeped over his garden wall. There he was, mowing the grass. There was a strong smell of newly mown grass. A large dog, a mastiff I think it was, looked up at me and growled. The man turned round and looked right at me. I felt safe enough, what with the huge brick wall between us, but he said something that sounded like Latin and pointed at the wall. A purple light seemed to cut a round hole through the wall and suddenly the dog was out at me, and me down the lane like you wouldn't believe. I didn't know that I could run that fast!'

'Did he bite you?' I asked, feeling slightly unsettled by this story.

'No. I heard the man shout a strange command. The dog stopped chasing me, turned round and ran back. I clearly saw the dog return back through the large hole in the wall.'

'Then what did you do?'

'I called the police, of course. They drove me to his house that night. A kindly looking gent opened the door and seemed surprised at my allegation. He said he didn't even own a dog.'

'Did you have the right property?'

'Yes. The name on the wall is "Melvin's Castle". Have a look as you go past.'

'Did you show the police the hole in the wall?' I said.

'I couldn't. We searched the garden, the police used their bright torches. The garden was completely surrounded by a wall with no holes whatsoever.'

'Then what did you do?'

'We went into the house to search for signs of a dog. The police and the man seemed to be losing their patience with me and must have thought that I had made the whole thing up. We didn't find any trace of a dog. But I did notice one thing.'

'What was that?' I asked. The train by this time had swept past and Steven started the procedure for opening the gates. I called to him, 'What did you notice?'

Steven finished opening the gates and walked back over to me. He looked around and leant forward again. 'A huge book on his shelf. It said *Ancient Magic*!'

Part 2

Suggestions for opening lines of stories:

1. The jungle did indeed produce some surprises, but the most amazing was to do with the banana tree spider.
2. I went to sleep and when I woke up I had changed into a teacup.
3. Every night, on the way home, I glanced in through the window. One night I didn't just get a shock, the experience changed the direction of the rest of my life.
5. Yes, I did get the chance to spend a year on a tropical island. I never would have guessed what was in store for me.
6. You might think that there is nothing particularly special about a boring old ordinary potato. But the one I'm going to tell you about actually saved my life.
7. They say that winning a lot of money makes you happy. Well, all I can say is that in my case it almost took my happiness away.
8. I had been patient and saved up all my money to buy that special dress. Who would have thought that it would have led to this?
9. I tried about 20 different jobs until, at last, by chance, I got this one. And I'll tell you something: I would never change it.
10. Yes, computers are amazing and all that. But listen to what happened when an old-fashioned notebook did what a computer could never do.

Story Telling Using Dialogue — **WORKSHEET**

Key skills

1. Writing about characters' viewpoints.

Starter

Ask students to write a list of ten places where adventurers might plan an expedition.

Ask students to write out in their own words the meaning of: 'optimist' and 'pessimist'.

Main phase

Part 1

Read through, with the students, the optimist's diary entries and discuss her attitude to her experiences.

Part 2

Read through, with the students, the pessimist's diary entries and discuss his attitude to his experiences.

Part 3

Ask students to choose one of the entries and continue the diary in the style of the writer.

Part 4

Ask students to look at the expedition suggestion list and choose one to write imaginative diary notes on. They are to choose an optimistic or a pessimistic attitude to their writing.

Plenary

Students' diary notes to be read out to the class.

Suggestions for homework

Ask students to do some research on a particularly hostile area of the world. Using the detailed information they have found, ask them to write a detailed diary note of an imaginative expedition.

Suggestions for development of this work

A class folder can be compiled with the expedition diaries separated into 'optimistic' and 'pessimistic'.

Extended exercise to develop a KS4 focus based on this work

Students to choose a destination and write two diary notes for the same expedition: one from an optimistic point of view, one from a pessimistic point of view. Compare them.

Extended exercise to develop a KS5 focus based on this work

Students to choose a destination and write two detailed and developed diary notes for the same expedition: one from an optimistic point of view, one from a pessimistic point of view. Compare them. Then students can produce a study under the heading of linguistic 'register' with a focus on 'linguistic field'. They are to extract the words and phrases which paint an optimistic field compared to those words and phrases which create a pessimistic field.

Part 1

Adelia had spent over a year planning an expedition across an inhospitable desert region. Here are extracts from some of her diary entires:

1 June

We trudged for miles today and I was amazed at the steady pace of the camels. They are wonderful creatures and there is something very comforting in their presence. Morale among my friends is mainly high. When their spirits fall I, as team leader, crack a joke or get them singing a song. That always seems to do the trick.

2 June

We hit a problem. One of the main water skins mysteriously sprung a leak and we are desperately short of water. I have complete confidence in our guide, Akio, in finding the next water hole in time. He is very experienced in these matters. More songs to keep up the morale. We have no choice but to just keep on going!

3 June

Yesterday evening we got a tiny bit concerned about the water situation, but sure enough, we found an oasis in the nick of time. I can't tell you how great that lovely fresh cool water tasted. Today is good solid progress. The colours in the desert are amazing.

4 June

This evening we found a wonderful shelter for the night, well out of the wind. If a sandstorm starts up, the only thing we can do is sit tight and wait it out. Akio is teaching me so much about this landscape. He feels it will turn into a sandstorm. If that happens, I shall use my special little torch under my blanket and read a good book!

5 June

Unfortunately a sandstorm did blow up. It has got in my hair, mouth, nose – everywhere. But let's look on the bright side. It won't last for ever, and it will be one of life's experiences that I can tell my grandchildren about one day. Oh yes, and I did manage to read a few pages of my book.

Part 2

Domingos has spent over a year planning an expedition to a jungle region, which includes a long river trip.

Here are extracts from some of his diary entries:

1 September

Terrifying. We had managed a couple of hundred yards paddling down the river when a huge river serpent nearly overturned our canoe. I knew this would happen! I wanted to go back. This is too dangerous. If I had thought more carefully in the planning stage, I would never have organized a river trip.

2 September

Our party is now trekking its way through the dense jungle. I should never have agreed to come to a jungle. There are spiders everywhere and at night the sound of things crawling about under the hammocks is simply horrifying. I want to go home. I hate every minute of this. I feel it's going to get worse.

3 September

I've had enough now and so I've demanded a helicopter to get me out of here, but our guide says that's impossible in such dense forest. What do I do? I've thrown a shouting fit and all that did was give me a headache! The others keep trying to cheer me up and say that it is a unique lifetime experience and adventure and all that stuff. I've told them to leave me alone and get lost!

4 September

I'm covered from head to toe with scratches and sweat. The guide tells me that I could easily get an infection if I don't dress the wounds. Just when I thought nothing else could go wrong. I've had to resort to opening my emergency 'Cheer up' letter from a loved one at home. I've read it. Cheer me up? I chucked it on the fire! I've never read such rubbish. 'Proud of me' and all that rubbish. How can she be proud of someone like me? All I want to do is go home before any more disasters strike me. By the way, the others seem quite cheerful. They must be raving mad to be cheerful in a place like this.

Part 3

Now choose one of the entries and continue the diary in the style of the writer.

Part 4

Choose from one of the following and write a diary entry deciding if the attitude should be optimistic or pessimistic:

1. A cycling trip across America.
2. An expedition to the South Pole.
3. An expedition to Easter Island in the Pacific Ocean.
4. An expedition to Mars.
5. An expedition into the deepest cave in the world.
6. An expedition to the highest mountain.
7. An expedition to the ocean bed.

Optimistic or Pessimistic Character? **WORKSHEET**

Key skills

1. Playwriting skills.
2. Language used in interview scenarios.

Starter

Ask students to write a list containing situations where a formal interview is required.

Main phase

Part 1

Allocate characters and read through the mini play entitled: 'Stargrace Hotel'.

Part 2

Read through the interview suggestions with the students and ask them to have a go at writing their own mini play based on the interview ideas. Or they could think up their own interview situation.

Tips: Remind them to think about the characters acting out the parts and add stage directions for the actors to use.

Explain to students that a strong attitude and viewpoint create a convincing character.

Make sure that any conflict is controlled and carefully managed. Never allow the action to degenerate into threats and violent behaviour.

Plenary

Read through and act out one of the student's plays to the rest of the class.

Suggestions for homework

Ask students to think of the person they would most like to meet from history. Ask them to write out an imaginary interview between the student and the person from history.

Suggestions for development of this work

Carry out the homework task above, with a different person from history, but add research to include detailed knowledge of that person's life.

Extended exercise to develop a KS4 focus based on this work

Students to write out the transcript of an interview between themselves and anyone they would wish to meet. They then rewrite the transcript in reported speech format for a short newspaper article.

Extended exercise to develop a KS5 focus based on this work

Carry out the exercise in KS4 above and in addition ask students to write an essay to answer this question: 'How does a reader respond to direct speech compared to reported speech?'

Part 1

Stargrace Hotel: A Stage Play

Characters: Joanne Linscott, the hotel receptionist; Mr Perkins, the hotel manager; Ms Jenkinson, the hotel owner.
Situation: The manager of Stargrace Hotel, Mr Perkins, calls the receptionist in for an interview.

Mr Perkins: Hello Joanne, I see you have my letter. Thank you for being punctual. Do take a seat.

Joanne: Thank you.

Mr Perkins: Now, I'll get straight to the point, Joanne. I'm very disappointed with you. (Pause) I've received a letter from none other than Mr Simon Symonds. (Holds up the letter) You know he's worth millions? He claims, and I have no reason to doubt his word, that you actually turned him away from our hotel on a cold and bitter night last week. Is this true?

Joanne: Yes, it is true.

Mr Perkins: (Stares at her with annoyance for a few moments, shows tension in the way he stands) Er . . . why was that? (Restrained annoyance in the voice)

Joanne: Because the rooms were full.

Mr Perkins: But Joanne, you know as well as I do that we keep the special room, the Diamond Suite, reserved for special people, don't we?

Joanne: Yes.

Mr Perkins: Then, what was the problem?

Joanne: The room was booked out.

Mr Perkins: The room was booked out? (Raising his voice)

Joanne: Yes.

Mr Perkins: Who to, for goodness sake?

Joanne: To Mr and Mrs Palmer. They're a lovely couple. They wanted a room, they had travelled far, the weather was awful, and they were willing to pay the going rate. (Pause, where they look at each other) . . . So I booked them in.

Mr Perkins: But that room is only for special customers.

Joanne: The way I see it, all customers are special.

Mr Perkins: You deliberately disobeyed my instructions. (Silence for a few moments. Joanne puts her head down) Well, I'm sorry to say that I'm going to serve a disciplinary letter on you. If you get another one, you're out and with that big mortgage you've just taken on, you'd better watch out!

Joanne: Please Mr Perkins, I've done nothing wrong. A customer is a customer.

Mr Perkins: You get paid to do as you're told. Now sign this letter to say you accept it!

Joanne: (Reads letter, then pushes it to one side) I request to see Ms Jenkinson.

Mr Perkins: Don't be silly. The owner of this hotel has got better things to do than waste time with silly little receptionists who disobey managers. Now sign here!

Joanne: (Rising anger) I demand to see Ms Jenkinson. I'm not moving from my seat until you get her.

Mr Perkins: (Stares at her as if he's about to burst. He then picks up the phone and dials a number) Oh, I'm sorry to disturb you, Madam. (Puts on a friendly, posh voice) Will you please just confirm that you don't want to be bothered with minor staff problems? (Pause) er . . . Joanne on reception . . . (Pause) yes er . . . upset a really important customer . . . er (Pause) . . . wants to see you . . . (Pause) Oh, I see. OK. Thank you. (Pause) She'll be here in a few moments.

(They wait, with awkward tension in the air. Enter Ms Jenkinson)

Mr Perkins: (Getting up from his seat) Ah, Ms Jenkinson, this is Joanne, and she's requested to see you.

Ms Jenkinson: I know Joanne, don't think I don't know who my own staff are! (Turns to Joanne with a friendly smile) Now dear, what can I do for you?

Mr Perkins: (Butts in) She's broken company policy and she's naturally being served the normal letter and she won't accept it.

Ms Jenkinson: I would like to speak to Joanne please, Mr Perkins. Now, tell me what happened.

Joanne: (Rushing her words) I thought all customers were important, so the other night I booked in a couple to the Diamond Suite. Then half an hour later I had to turn away Mr Simon Symonds and he's complained to Mr Perkins, and now Mr Perkins wants to give me a disciplinary letter and I'm worried about my mortgage and . . .

Ms Jenkinson: Wait a moment, wait a moment. Mr Perkins, what appears to be the problem with what Joanne did?

Mr Perkins: Well Madam, you know we keep the special suite for special customers and . . .

Ms Jenkinson: What rubbish! If a customer can pay, that's fine by me. Tell Mr Symonds to come and see me if he's got a problem with that. As for Joanne here, well, she's highly regarded by both colleagues and customers. She works hard. I will not have her upset, do you hear me? It's you who should be getting a disciplinary, not her. Now, I don't want to hear another word. Please leave the room Mr Perkins.

Mr Perkins: But I thought . . .

Ms Jenkinson: No buts . . . just go please, I want a quiet word with this young girl. (Perkins exits) Now Joanne, two things. First of all, if that brute of a man causes you trouble over this, let me know straight away. Second, if you are worried about your mortgage, come and see me. I'm sure we can sort something out. I don't want my good staff to be worried about money.

Joanne: Thank you, Ms Jenkinson. Thank you so very much.

Part 2

Suggestions for interview scenarios:

1. An employee is interviewed for suspected theft of cash from the till.
2. A police detective interviews a suspect regarding a serious crime.
3. A young woman TV presenter interviews a famous actor on a TV chat show.
4. A news reporter interviews a woman who has acted heroically and saved someone's life.
5. A bank manager interviews a young entrepreneur who wants to borrow money to open up a new night club.
6. A chosen student interviews an astronaut who will explain what it was like to walk on the moon.
7. A reporter interviews a new rock band who are fast becoming famous.

The Interview **WORKSHEET**

Key skills

1. Describing character.

Starter

Ask students to consider the following:

Imagine a hot day on the beach. For each of the following, write a sentence to express how each character feels. The first one is done as a guide:

1. Young child: 'I can't wait until I can have an ice cream.'
2. Old person.
3. Lifeguard.
4. A large dog.
5. A police officer on duty.
6. A teenager with a group of friends.
7. The owner of an ice-cream kiosk.

Main phase

Part 1

Read through with the class the tasks on the worksheet. Discuss how a viewpoint can give an insight into a character.

Part 2

Read through the situations on the suggestion list and ask students to choose from the list and write a series of viewpoints from the characters involved in the style of the worked example. Remind them that although the situation is the same for each character in that scenario, the way they see it and think about it may be completely different.

Plenary

Ask students to read out their situations and variety of viewpoints.

Suggestions for homework

Ask students to pick another scenario from the situations list and encourage them to spend more time thinking in detail about the various possible viewpoints and write out more fully a variety of characters' viewpoints.

Suggestions for development of this work

Ask students to pick a situation from Part 2, which they haven't worked on yet, and write out detailed diary notes from the point of view of one or more of the characters in the situation, reflecting on the event and revealing thoughts and feelings.

Extended exercise to develop a KS4 focus based on this work

Ask students to pick a situation from Part 2, which they haven't worked on yet, and write out a letter from the point of view of one or more of the characters in the situation, to be sent to a friend, reflecting on the event explaining what happened.

Extended exercise to develop a KS5 focus based on this work

Ask students to get into small groups and pick a situation from Part 2, which they haven't worked on yet, and write out a letter from the point of view of one or more of the characters in the situation, to be sent to a friend, reflecting on the event explaining what happened. Then get them to arrange a role play where the group meets up to discuss the event. Make a comparison between the written letters and the discussions. What are the similarities and differences?

Part 1

Task 1. Imagine the following situation. A travelling circus has arrived in town and set up the big top in a large field. Tonight the performance starts at 7 pm. At 6.45 pm the following people are involved in this situation:

A clown is sitting in his caravan putting on his make-up.

A young woman is working in the ticket caravan selling tickets to the queues of customers.

The owner (who is also the Ringmaster) is wandering around, checking that everything is ready.

The strong man is preparing himself for his performance.

In the queue a man stands with his children waiting to get tickets.

A group of teenage girls stand excited in the queue.

An elderly retired couple wait patiently in the queue.

Task 2. Imagine the thought processes of each character (this is known as the internal monologue) in response to the situation they are in:

Clown:	Here we go again; I must forget that bill I can't pay. I must give another great performance tonight; I just hope that Rocco, my fellow clown, gets his timing right tonight. Last night he was all over the place!
Ticket seller:	Thank goodness the queue is long tonight. I'm going to have to really rush and change my costume after I've finished here. Oh dear, I feel exhausted already, having helped put the big top up yet again. Still, the show must go on!
The owner:	Well, everyone seems to be ready. I'm really pleased with them all. They put that top up in record time. And that queue, it's great. We need some good takings. It's been down a bit lately. Hopefully I might be able to give them bit of a bonus this time, they need of a morale boost! Better check up on my daughter in the ticket office, she looked so tired earlier, hope she'll be all right tonight.
The strong man:	I can't believe I'm still doing this at my age; it's getting harder – but what else can I do? Here comes the boss – I'd better look lively . . .
Man with children in queue:	Wow, this looks popular! I've not been to the circus for years, I'm getting quite excited, it's as if I'm a child again. My kids! Look at their faces, I should have brought my camera.
Child in queue:	Those flashing, bright-coloured lights are great. Where's the clown? I've never seen so many caravans. They're all different. This grass is all muddy. Where is the candy floss? That music is loud . . . isn't this great?

Part 2

Variety of situations and characters:

Situation	Characters in the situation
Minor accident on the road.	Driver. Ambulance paramedic on the scene. Police officer. Witness.
Pop concert.	Famous performer. Member of audience. Support staff. Hot-dog vendor.
Carnival procession.	Member of one of the floats. Someone dressed up as a bear. Organizer. Child in crowd. Adult in the crowd. Sweet-shop owner open late.

Viewpoints Reveal Character **WORKSHEET**

Key skills

1. Writing to explain.
2. Variety of writing activities based on a theme.

Starter

Ask students for ten minutes to write a list of things which annoy them.

Main phase

Part 1

Read through with students the examples list of things which can annoy.

Part 2

Ask students to write their own list of things which annoy them, this time expanding the details of their explanations, in the style of the examples in Part 1 of the worksheet.

Part 3

Read through the 'letter to editor' example which explains something which annoys the reader in more detail.

Ask students to write their own letter to the editor for the column entitled 'What Annoys You?' in an imaginary favourite magazine. Ask them to base it on the style of the example.

Part 4

Ask students to choose from the list one of the writing activities which features something which annoys them. They may wish to choose from the list or think up their own writing task.

Plenary

Ask students to read their work to each other and discuss reactions to it.

Suggestions for homework

Ask students to compile a list from family members to include what annoys them. They can then bring the list to the next lesson to share ideas.

Suggestions for development of this work

Arrange for the class to produce a magazine section entitled: 'What Annoys our Readers' and compile a collection of articles. Have them typed up and presented in the style of a magazine. Allocate a task for each member of the group. For example: editor; cartoon; puzzle section; illustrations, etc.

Extended exercise to develop a KS4 focus based on this work

Ask students to research a wide variety of magazines and write a list of common features of the 'Letters to editor' sections.

Extended exercise to develop a KS5 focus based on this work

Ask students to research and arrange interviews with various teachers with the aim of writing an essay called: 'What is it that annoys teachers most?'

Part 1

A list of things which can annoy:

1. Not being able to get the cellophane off of a packet of biscuits (especially if you're hungry).
2. Sitting in a cinema next to someone who smells.
3. Being in a hurry and meeting a neighbour who insists on a chat.
4. Waiting at the till in a shop and an assistant ignores you (or carries on a conversation with a colleague about what happened the night before!).
5. Waiting for an important letter, watching the postman arrive, and finding that the letter still isn't there.
6. Chatting to a friend and then noticing in the mirror, a little while later, that you have a bit of food on your face near to your mouth.
7. Telling a bit of a fib and someone with you corrects you.
8. Thinking that there is one last sweet in your bag and discovering that actually you ate it.
9. Spending hours working on a computer and then losing all your work.
10. Pressing the remote for the TV and finding that the battery has gone.

Part 2

Write your own list of things which annoy you in the style of the example list in Part 1.

Part 3

Example of a letter to the editor:

Dear Editor,

I am writing in reply to your request for letters from readers on the subject of 'What Annoys You?'.

My annoyance concerns complaints. If you purchase an unsatisfactory product or service and you ring up to complain (only after pressing button after button after button and listening to ridiculous amounts of utterly irrelevant information – but that's a separate annoyance), you eventually speak to someone in some call centre somewhere who shows not the slightest concern about your complaint. But here comes the really annoying part. They refer you casually to their 'Complaints Department' as if they are so used to complaints that it is just another one. Complaining used to be a serious matter, these days it seems quite normal and expected. Has customer service really got so bad generally?

Yours sincerely

Dexter Burfoot

Decide on your own annoying thing and write a letter to the editor in the style of the example.

Part 4

Ideas for short writing activities based on the theme of: 'What annoys you?'.

1. Two friends discuss what annoys them about the little things in life. Write a dialogue.
2. Write about a day, in the form of a diary note, where one thing after another annoyed you.
3. Write a piece of advice, suitable for a magazine, entitled 'Don't let little things annoy you. How to stay calm and happy'.
4. Write out a description of a dream where lots of annoying things happened. Use the style of free-flowing writing.
5. Write a letter to a shop explaining clearly why you were annoyed when you visited it.
6. Write a short poem, in any style, entitled: 'What Annoys Me!'
7. Write a short radio drama entitled 'The Annoying Thing' and show how various characters react to a source of annoyance.

What Annoys You? **WORKSHEET**

Section J: Time

Key skills
1. Writing to explain.
2. Writing to engage the interest of the reader.

Starter

Ask students to write down the most amazing thing that they have ever found out in their life.

For example: as a child, the discovery of the amazing taste of cream soda; the discovery that two microscopic cells join to then divide and eventually form a human being; the fact that space stretches on for ever and ever; the discovery that time keeps on going.

Main phase

Part 1
Read through with the class the story in the worksheet entitiled: 'Daisy's discoveries'.

Part 2
Ask students to write their own story about an amazing discovery, basing it on the style of the example.

Plenary

Ask students to read their stories to each other and discuss strong points and areas to improve on.

Suggestions for homework

Ask students to research famous discoveries and produce an information sheet detailing key points in their own words.

Suggestions for development of this work

Arrange a display where the various discoveries can be displayed with colourful and lively illustrations.

Extended exercise to develop a KS4 focus based on this work

Students to review from the selection of important and famous discoveries done for homework and then choose one. They are then to imagine that they are the person who actually made the discovery and then write about it at the point of discovery. Ask them to include as much detail as possible to make it seem real and to bring it alive. They base it on facts but create a fictionalized story where imaginative things are added to create interest in the reader.

Extended exercise to develop a KS5 focus based on this work

Students to carry out the activity as in the KS4 Focus and in addition write a factual article for a magazine and then compare it to their fictionally enhanced account. They then write an essay to answer this question: 'Look carefully at your fictionalized account of the famous discovery and compare it to the factual article. What are the similarities and differences of the two pieces of writing?'

Daisy's discoveries

Daisy held the large packages tightly and ran through the crowds of Cambridge towards the elegant room of her professor. She nearly barged a porter out of the way as she ran up the ancient stairway. She hardly knocked on the door and flew in, panting. Professor Green had his back to her and was gazing out of the window across the quad.

'Look, professor. You must be the first to see these,' she cried. The professor, who had been deep in thought, was quite shocked. He had worked with Daisy for a number of years now on their various historical investigations, and he had grown accustomed to her sudden bursts of excitement. But this was a level of excitement he had never seen before.

'Daisy, Daisy, calm down for heaven's sake. Please.' He waved his pipe at the chair for her to sit.

'Professor, this could be quite the most important find in history ever!' Daisy was beaming with excitement. Her eyes were sparkling. 'Look at these!' She spread out a set of old documents on the table. The professor picked one up and studied it. He placed it back on the table and then picked up another, then another.

'Yes, they're interesting historical re-enactment photographs. Where did you buy them?' he asked in a fairly dismissive voice.

'No, professor. They are not re-enactment photographs. Look at this one.' She picked up one of the documents. 'See the woman holding the wooden bucket?'

'Yes, it's in the style of a Viking woman.'

'Well, I've just got back from the lab and they've verified the day of this document. Its AD 725!'

'Well, someone has got hold of an old document and used a process to superimpose a picture onto it,' his voice was still casual.

'No. Read this.' She handed the professor a piece of paper. He read it out loud:

'The ink used is primitive animal pigment and is textured into the fibres of the vellum at the time of AD 725. Signed, lab manager.' He read and looked at her. 'Daisy, it's some sort of clever fake, or hoax. If you remember, the camera wasn't invented until about 1830.' His voice remained calm and uninterested.

'Really, professor. Then what about this . . .' From the other package she produced a strange little wooden box, of obvious great age, and handed it over delicately. For the first time the professor began to look interested.

'That has been examined and carefully dated. It is authentic and was made in AD 715. It has everything you need to take a photograph. Professor, you are looking at a camera made by the Vikings!' The Professor returned to the documents on the table. He picked them up slowly and examined them with a sudden intensity of interest.

'Where were these found?' he asked, his voice now very serious.

'These were found at Colchester three days ago. Now, are you ready for the next one?' She looked at him. He was becoming slightly overwhelmed by now. She took some more documents from the package and handed them to him.

'But this is a picture of the Roman temple at Colchester.' There was quite a pause. 'You're not telling me that the Romans had cameras too?'

'They didn't just have cameras. Look at this, but brace yourself first.' Out of the package came another object which was extremely old and falling to pieces. It consisted of bits of wood and bits of metal. 'This, professor, believe it or not, is a moving film camera dating from Roman times.' The professor handled it carefully and was obviously overwhelmed.

'Professor, I now have in my hand perhaps the most significant historical find of all time. The technicians, by a very special painstaking process, and by working all night, were able to identify fragments of moving film material and with the aid of special equipment and computer programs were able to make a copy and put it onto this computer. I would now like you to watch a 57-second sequence film of Colchester. The date? AD 200!'

Daisy opened up a laptop and pressed a few buttons. A brown, flickering image appeared on the screen. The quality improved as a few seconds went by. There on the screen were Romans building a wall.

Key skills

1. Writing an archaeologist's style report.
2. Exploring the effects of time.

Starter

Ask students to look around the room they are in and imagine what might, in 300 years, still survive. For example, an exercise book would most probably rot away and leave no trace (except maybe the staples), whereas a plastic board writer may still exist.

Ask them to compile a list and next to each item jot down a description of what it might look like.

For example:

1. White board; little small fragments remain, now black but still with a smooth surface.

Main phase

Part 1

Read the Archaeologist's Report for an account of the archaeologists finding the remains of a theatre in 300 years' time and trying to guess what each item is. In 300 years it will be an entirely different world, so the remains of the theatre will present a mystery to interpret. Briefly discuss the account with the class. Point out the mystery in understanding the remains of each item.

Part 2

Read through this section with the students and ask them to choose a location and then write a site report in the style of the example in Part 1.

Plenary

Ask a few students to read out their reports and ask others in the class to see if they can guess the location.

Suggestions for homework

Select a scenario and draw a 'site plan' as if you were an archaeologist of the future. Draw an image of each item and label it with words in red to show how it originally was, for example, brown leather football, and in black how it is 300 years on; for example, a few black strips remain of very thin leather; a few stitches remain.

Suggestion for development of this work

Ask students to do this task: 'Imagine that you are transported 300 years into the future. Write a detailed description of what you see.'

Extended exercise to develop a KS4 focus based on this work

Ask students to do this task: 'Research a period of history many hundreds of years ago. Imagine that you are transported back through time 600 years. The place is where you are now. Write a detailed description of what you might see.'

Extended exercise to develop a KS5 focus based on this work

Ask students to do this task: 'Research a period of history many hundreds of years ago. Imagine that you are transported back through time 600 years. The place is where you are now. Write a description of what you might see. Then, with the aid of your research, write a page of factual information about the period for an encyclopaedia. Compare the two texts and write an essay answering this question: How do the two texts use language in different ways?'

Part 1

Archaeologists' report

Location: Colminster
Date: 1 August 2309
Site reference number: 12345
Condition of soil: Peaty and therefore very good preservation qualities.

Find 1 Description (actually a small part of a rehearsal floor marked out with white tape)
The item is about a quarter of a square metre and is smooth on one side with strange white tape arranged in weird patterns.
Possible explanation: We think that the tape was deliberately arranged in this way and may well have been a piece of what was once known as 'modern art' or a religious symbol of some sort.

Find 2 Description (actually a microphone with different coloured electrical wires attached)
The item is 12 centimetres long and is cylindrical with a diameter of 4 centimetres. One end is shaped like the ancient pictures of ice cream cones we found at other sites.
Possible explanation: We think it could be a sculpture of an ice cream cone. Maybe ice cream had special significance in those days?

Find 3 Description (actually a First World War soldier's uniform from the costume department)
We have carefully examined the remains of this fabric and we have found green threads and buttons made of brass.
Possible explanation: We think it might be some kind of military clothing. It might suggest that this is in fact the scene of a battle.

Find 4 Description (actually large artificial diamonds for costume jewellery)
We have carried out various scientific tests on these items. They have the appearance of diamonds but are made of a common manufactured substance. Perhaps the people who lived here were poor and could not afford real diamonds?

Part 2

Imagine that you are part of a team of archaeologists 300 years in the future. You are digging up sites of various kinds and trying to make sense of the decayed finds which turn up. Remember, in 300 years the world will be very different from how it is now.

Here is a list of possible sites which you could uncover. Note that in your report the actual identification of the artefact is given, even though as archaeologists of the future you can only describe what you actually see and you make an assumption about what it may have been. Remember that things which are obvious to us now will be extremely mysterious in the future.

Possible sites to choose from:

1. A zoo.
2. Nightclub.
3. Factory.
4. Shop.
5. Football stadium.
6. Hospital.
7. Theatre.
8. A circus.
9. A leisure and sports centre.

Choose a location from the list above and make a list of items which would commonly be associated with it.

Against each item write a brief description of how it might look 300 years from now.

Now, write an archaeologist's report in the style of the worked example. The key focus here is to imagine how an item which we are familiar with today might mystify the people of the future. Include some possible guesses about the item which can be included in the report.

Future Remains **WORKSHEET**

Key skills

1. Descriptive and highly imaginative writing.

Starter

Ask students to write a description of what they think the world will be like in 1,000 years' time.

Main phase

Part 1
Read through with students the examples of ideas for the future list on the worksheet, and discuss.

Part 2
Ask students to write their own list in the style of the examples in Part 1.

Part 3
Read through the range of writing activities and ask students to choose one and write a developed piece of writing based on their ideas about the future.

Plenary

Ask students to read their written ideas to each other.

Suggestions for homework

Ask students to draw a picture of how the future will look and ask them to add written detailed labels to it.

Suggestions for development of this work

Arrange the completion of a class file to be called '1,000 Years from Now – What Will Life be Like?' Allocate each student a different task so that when they are all put together they will create a wholesome and imaginative view of the future.

Examples of tasks: Describe food; clothes; transport; entertainment; weather; towns; armies, etc.

See if it can be arranged so that the students choose what they want to do.

You may wish to include in the file a whole range of written activities and illustrations.

Extended exercise to develop a KS4 focus based on this work

Ask students to write a fully detailed essay entitled: 'Life in 1,000 Years' Time'.

Extended exercise to develop a KS5 focus based on this work

Ask students to write a fully detailed essay entitled: 'Life in 1,000 Years' Time'. Then arrange for students to work together and read each other's essays and write critical commentaries suggesting areas to edit, develop and improve. Students to then rewrite their essays in the light of the critical commentaries.

Part 1

Examples of how the future might be in 1,000 years' time:

1. Buildings maybe will be constructed in such a way that they 'read' your thought patterns and automatically adjust and serve you. E.g.: temperature and light control, background music to suit your mood in an instant.
2. Food. A robot servant will have stored in its computer brain every bit of medical information about you so that the food can be matched 100 per cent to your needs and desires.
3. Clothes. These will be projected onto you from a maze of laser type projectors in such an accurate way that you can wear whatever you want, whenever you want. They will look and feel exactly like traditional clothes but can be altered and changed to anything in an instant.
4. Information. Fitted to peoples' heads will be tiny nano chips so that by simply thinking a question the answer will be fed automatically from a super worldwide computer which contains all knowledge known to the human race.

Part 2

Write out and explain your own ideas for the future in the style of the examples in Part 1.

Part 3

Writing activities:

1. Imagine you are alive 1,000 years from now. Write a diary entry for one day in the life of yourself, based on the ideas for the future list, or based on your own ideas.
2. Imagine you are alive 1,000 years from now. Write a description of what you can see.
3. Imagine you had a powerfully vivid dream about the future. Write out the dream, including images from the future, in a flow of consciousness style of writing.
4. Write the script for a mini play set 1,000 years from now.
5. Write a poem about the future in any style you wish to use.

What does the Future Hold? **WORKSHEET**

Key skills

1. Developing writing about memories.

Starter

Ask students to write down a description of a memory which stands out for them.

Main phase

Part 1

Read through the two examples on the worksheet where a man looks back at his holiday years ago when he was a small child before decimalization and when they still had steam trains. Point out to the students that the first example is a basic account. This is produced by just a rapid thinking about the memory and a jotting down of main points.

Explain to the students that he then goes over the writing again and embellishes and develops the details to transform the writing.

Ask the students to compare the two drafts and identify the differences.

Part 2

Ask students to pick a memory from the starter they did and to write it out in the quick plain style of Draft 1.

Part 3

Ask students to rewrite and transform by adding details to their first draft as in the worked example. Remind them to use the checklist to prompt ideas.

Plenary

Ask students to read to the class their first draft and then their enhanced second draft. Ask students to comment on the experience of listening to the first one compared to the second.

Suggestions for homework

Ask students to spend some quiet peaceful time at home to write out a first draft of another memory of theirs. Ask them to bring the draft to the next lesson so that more time can be spent in the next lesson on writing a really good-quality enhanced draft.

Suggestions for development of this work

1. Ask students to chat to a family member and see if they will agree to share a vivid memory.
2. Students then jot down key points and notes.
3. From the notes they then produce a brief first draft.
4. From the first draft they then produce an enhanced draft, adding details.
5. Ask the family member to read the enhanced draft and write a comment on it.

Extended exercise to develop a KS4 focus based on this work

Ask students to read out their own written memories and then do a Speaking and Listening session with the class to explain, describe and narrate extra details about the memories.

Extended exercise to develop a KS5 focus based on this work

Imagine a Remembrance Day article in a newspaper where an old war veteran recalls his memories. Ask students to research and produce such an article which quotes from the veteran's memories.

Now produce a variety of possible headlines for the article and comment on how they produce a sense of drama.

Part 1

My holiday with my nan in New Milton – first draft (basic straightforward account)

When I was about seven I was sent down to stay for a couple of weeks with my nan. She was just wonderful. I remember her smiling face. She always spoilt me. We travelled by train and I still remember the smell of the smoke from the steam engine. As we approached the forest I can remember looking out at the trees and the setting sun. The railway station made such a deep impression on me at New Milton. We stopped at a Cadbury's chocolate machine where nan bought me some chocolate. My nan let me eat the chocolate all in one go.

'Greengables' was a large house and my nan had a room in it. I remember the huge white doors. There was a grandfather clock and it had a loud tick-tock. The smell was like polish. My nan also used lavender perfume.

My holiday with my nan in New Milton – second draft (with added details)

When I was about seven I was sent down to the New Forest to stay a couple of weeks with my nan. How can I describe her? She was just wonderful. I remember her smiling face and her floral dress. She always spoilt me. Spoilt me more than anyone could ever imagine.

We travelled by train and I still remember the smell of the smoke from the steam engine. Then there was the shunt, shunt, shunt, and the shudder of the carriages. As we approached the forest I can remember a twinge of homesickness as I looked out across the yellow glades between the trees as the setting sun sent long golden shadows – which still gives me pleasure to remember now.

The railway station made such a deep impression on me at New Milton that to this day I still regard old railway stations as places of magic and wonder. We stopped at a Cadbury's chocolate machine where nan put a shilling in and a huge bar was delivered into a tray at the bottom. The really great thing about my nan was the way she let me eat the chocolate all in one go. No moaning; no 'You've got to eat your dinner first' comments. She just smiled as I munched on.

'Greengables' was a large house set in a massive garden and my nan had a room in it. I remember the huge doors (perhaps it was just that I was so small) and if I think about it the white paint seemed so thickly laid on the wood. There was a grandfather clock and the tick-tock was so loud that it still sounds out somewhere in my memory. I can hear it now as I write this. Now I'm going to try to describe the smell of the place. I know I shall fail miserably but I shall try. It was like polish and dust and old wood and fruit and flowers all rolled into one amazing beautiful wonderful smell. Oh, that's right – and perfume, lavender perfume. I can't smell lavender without remembering my nan.

Part 2

Write out a basic first draft of some memories you've had. Try to use the style and form of Draft 1 in the example above. You may wish to look at some ideas produced in your starter or you may wish to think up a new one.

Part 3

Rewrite the first draft and add details to make your own memories more vivid, as in the worked example.

Use this checklist to prompt ideas:

Who did you go with?	Anything scary?
Where did you go?	Anything lovely or enjoyable?
When was this?	What thoughts did you have?
Describe the journey.	How much did it cost?
How old were you?	Clothes?
What things did you buy?	Toys and games?
What smells do you remember?	Walks?
What sights do you recall?	Shops?
What sounds did you hear?	Cinema?
Did you meet new friends?	Eats?
Anything unusual?	Sweets and nice things?
People?	Drinks?
What did you learn?	

Transforming the Memories   **WORKSHEET**

135

Key skills

1. Writing to describe.

Starter

Set the students this task: If time could be suddenly frozen for one hour, and everyone in your school was frozen in time and space, except you, describe what you would see as you wandered round at this moment.

Main phase

Part 1

Read through with students Part 1 of the worksheet 'A Moment in Time'. Discuss with students that they are little impressions of what is happening at that moment. Point out that the narrative technique is based on the style of the beginning of *Under Milk Wood* by Dylan Thomas, where the narrator leads the reader by the hand, almost as if he is physically taking him round and showing him things.

Ask students to notice the following about the writing:

1. It is in the present tense.
2. It gives little hints and allows the rest of the image to grow in the reader's mind. It is not too descriptive.
3. Its focus of vision moves on from place to place.
4. It includes a variety of places.
5. It adds interest by the narrator, at points, where consideration is given to what the person might be thinking
6. It includes connecting phrases to draw the reader along, like 'Look over there'; 'Come with me'.

Part 2

Read the suggestions through with the students and ask them to choose one of the suggested situations from the list and write about it in full using the style of the example in Part 1.

Plenary

Students to read out their work and members of the class try to work out which location is being written about.

Suggestions for homework

Ask students to find an interesting picture which includes a lot of people. They are to write about what is happening, in detail, at that moment in time, in the picture.

Suggestions for development of this work

Students to produce a short mime play based on one of their scenes. They then role-play the characters as the narrator reads the parts which apply to them. It works well if they freeze-frame while the words that actually apply to them are read. They then melt away while the next characters loom up, to give the impression of moving through a scene. It's best to experiment and run it through a few times, trying out different approaches.

Extended exercise to develop a KS4 focus based on this work

Students to produce a story board of their scene. Underneath each picture they write a caption to match, taken and adapted from the writing.

Extended exercise to develop a KS5 focus based on this work

Students to read the opening part of *Under Milk Wood* by Dylan Thomas and then prepare a dramatic presentation where a variety of voices is used. The students then write a detailed and full answer to this question: 'How does the language of the opening of *Under Milk Wood* draw in the reader's attention and interest?'

Part 1

Five o'clock

Five o'clock in the afternoon. Listen. Can you hear the postman jangling his keys and swinging open that heavy, red, metal door? Look. The letters tumble out and the large hands gather them into the worn sack. 'Wow, that's a bit full.' And there, over the road, see the tired young woman yawning and starting the process of wheeling those awkward trolleys of shoes back into the shop. She gives the impression that she's done that a few times. Oh dear, a few shoes have dropped off, but her face seems to say: 'Shall I go out tonight?'

Now follow me as we stroll past the next shop where that butcher is washing down his stainless steel display. What a stench of detergent! Now, he is looking up at us with a weary eye. Oh, it is a very weary, bloodshot eye, isn't it? His face seems to say: 'I do hope you're not a customer, I've had enough today.' Look at his apron. To think that that was white and clean this morning.

Let's walk along a bit further and see what's happening in the bus queue. One man is glancing at his watch, another is checking the money in his wallet. Oh, doesn't he look worried? An elderly woman painfully transfers her weight from leg to leg. Her whole being is saying: 'Whenever will that bus come? I need a cup of tea.'

If you turn the corner and come with me, I will show you a nice little cafe, all brightly lit up. And look, they still have a few customers. Smell that. I think it's toasted tea cakes. See there, the man with a tiny moustache and a huge belly wiping down a table and whistling a tune. He is almost dancing around the cafe, and doesn't he seem to be saying: 'Quite a few customers . . . not a bad day.'

Let's stroll up to the library, shall we? What a depressing-looking building. The library bus has just arrived back from its rounds and is reversing in. See the harassed lady at the wheel? What is that she is shouting to the waiting librarian? 'Traffic was bad. One more year to retirement.' She is laughing a lot, see her? But I bet she means it. I bet she isn't laughing on the inside.

Come with me and look, look through the window of the estate agents. Do you see that man with rolled-up sleeves? See how he chats on the phone and gesticulates with his hands? Well, whenever I look in there he does that. He seems a little stressed and worried tonight though, doesn't he? Over there, is that a roadsweeper outside that newsagent's, pausing for a second and examining an advert in the window? Notice how he sighs. And notice too, how heavily he leans on his broom.

And what does he think he's playing at, right up there? What is he doing, with nobody holding his ladder? Oh, I see, as we get closer can you see what he's doing? He's putting a new tile on that roof. He's a long way up, isn't he?

Part 2

Situations to write 'A moment in time' impression about:

A walk around:

1. A zoo.
2. A leisure centre.
3. An airport.
4. A park.
5. A railway station.

6. A holiday camp.
7. A supermarket.
8. A vet's surgery.
9. A camping site.
10. A theme park.

A Moment in Time   **WORKSHEET**

Key skills

1. Writing to describe.
2. Writing to a theme.

Starter

Ask students to describe the following, comparing when they were new to after a lapse of time, as shown.

1. A fresh orange, then after six weeks.
2. A new car, then after 50 years.
3. A newly built house, then after 100 years.
4. A new pair of shoes, then after ten years.

Main phase

Part 1

Read the worksheet 'Market day'.

Discussion point: To capture the essence of a scene, pick out a few typical aspects and write about them, noticing little details to fix things in the reader's mind. Most readers already know what a market looks like, and so your writing needs really just to 'remind' them by using a few examples of what is there and by focusing onto particular details.

Part 2

Ask students to carry out an 'appeal to the senses' test. Go through 'Market day' and identify any reference to the five senses. Discussion point: Explain to students that by appealing to more than just the sense of sight, it brings the scene alive in the reader's mind.

Part 3

Ask students to look at the 'List of ideas to compare changes over a time period' on the worksheet. Ask them to choose one. Now ask them to write a full and detailed description of the scene at the beginning and then at the end of a time period, trying to model the style on the worked example.

Working method: a good working method to teach them is to write out a list of typical things that may be typically there at the scene and then concentrate on each item, thinking about how it may change over the time period.

Remind them to try to include specific details and sights, sounds, smells and even the taste of things if possible.

Plenary

Students to read out their own descriptions to the class.

Suggestions for homework

Students to think up their own scenarios where a situation at the start could be compared to the situation after a passage of time. Ask students to think of one and write out a full and detailed description, in the style of the example.

Suggestions for development of this work

A wall display could be produced with pictures of a variety of things during various timescales and extracts from descriptions, in the style of the example, on the students' worksheet.

Extended exercise to develop a KS4 focus based on this work

Ask students to prepare thoroughly and then write a full and detailed answer to this:
'Write a description of how a town you know well looks today and how it might look in 100 years from now.'

Extended exercise to develop a KS5 focus based on this work

Ask students to research the writing of Thomas Hardy and find a description where he has written about the effect of time on a scene. The students are then to write an essay in response to this question: 'How does Hardy, in the passage you have chosen, use language skilfully to show the effects of the passing of time?'

Part 1

Market day

Imagine a busy market in full swing on a hot summer's day. How would it look?

Market in full swing

There would be market callers yelling out: 'Lovely strawberries, two for a pound!' There'd be a sense of a great throng of people sauntering around, picking up things, handling them and moving on. The market traders would be watching the customers, eyes everywhere, eager to sell something. Stalls would have their brightly coloured wares arranged neatly for display. Fluorescent price stickers would be everywhere. Children would be asking mummy for some irresistible pink-coloured sweets. The music from radios would be playing happy, loud songs to make everyone feel good. Customers' faces everywhere would be showing the mental decision-making processes: 'To buy or not to buy?' You can imagine hundreds of other 'typical' things that you would see at a market in full swing.

Market at the end of the day

In the air is the loud exaggerated laughter of relief that the work is nearly done. Strewn on the floor are bits of fruit and vegetables; empty wooden packing cases are piled up; traders are sloshing water with a smell of disinfectant around the ground. A last few straggling customers are ferreting around; traders are offering ridiculous last-minute bargains: 'Go on love, you can have the whole lot for a pound!' The radio is blaring out news items or football results. Traders are bantering around in mock fights. Vans have been backed in from all over, and white doors are swung open as stock is unceremoniously thrown in. There is the clanking of metal frames being dismantled, and the boredom and tedium is etched on tired, sunburned faces. Hanging in the air is the heavy smell of fish. There is an undeniable sense of energy and hurry towards a finishing point.

Part 2

Read through 'Market day' again and copy out where descriptions effect the five senses of sight, smell, hearing, taste and feel.

Part 3

List of ideas to compare changes over a time period:

1. The beginning of a football match compared to the end.
2. The early stages of a building site compared to the finished building.
3. The early part of a school trip compared to the end.
4. The beginning of a play at the theatre, from as the audience enter, to the end of the play.
5. The first day at school compared to the last.
6. The first day at a new job compared to the day before retirement.
7. A young soldier in training compared to when he is a retired soldier talking about his career.

How Time Changes Things **WORKSHEET**

62786

Printed in Great Britain
by Amazon.co.uk, Ltd.,
Marston Gate.